A
AM

AFRICAN AMERICAN MALES

A Critical Link in the African American Family

Dionne J. Jones, editor

Transaction Publishers
New Brunswick (U.S.A.) and London (U.K.)

Library of Congress Catalog Number: 94-2281
ISBN: 1-56000-744-3
Printed in the United States of America

Library of Congress Cataloging-in-Publication Data

African American males : a critical link in the African American family / edited by Dionne J. Jones.
    p. cm.
    "Previously published in The Urban League review, 1993, volume 16, number 2"—T.p. verso.
    Includes bibliographical references.
    ISBN 1-56000-744-3
    1. Afro-American men. 2. Afro-American families. I. Jones, Dionne J.
E185.86.A334 1994
305.38'896073—dc20
                                                94-2281
                                                  CIP

Contents

Introduction

Dionne J. Jones

African American families have demonstrated their strengths[1] and survival skills through many generations, from slavery to the present time. Historicallly, they have faced tremendous hardships and have survived against all odds. As the African American middle class has grown over the last two decades, so have their numbers of elected officials and businesses. Median family income for African Americans increased from $20,103 in 1980 to $21,423 in 1990. Yet, this figure represented only 58 percent of the median income for white families in 1990.[2]

Today, African American men, women and their children are experiencing extreme stress. This cuts across class lines. Adults are concerned about the security of their jobs and at the same time, they are worried about their children's future. With the official Department of Labor (DOL) unemployment rates among African Americans reaching as high as 14.9 percent in 1992 (24.9% according to the National Urban League's Hidden Unemployment Index) and 39.8 percent among African American teenagers (44.3% HUI), there is cause for despair among many families.[3] Such economic disparities create barriers to social mobility and facilitate engagement in antisocial and illegal activities.

African American parents worry about their children's ability to survive in a hostile world. They worry about what the schools are doing to them or not doing for them. They worry about a criminal justice system that seems ever so quick to penalize their children both with and without due process. They worry about the conditions established by the wider society to instill fear and castigation of African American youth.

A national survey of children and parents conducted recently by the National Commission on Children concluded that minority parents more than other parents, experience extreme and frequent fear and worry about their children's physical safety and well being.[4] African American parents were one and one-half to three times as likely as white parents to report that they worry that their teenagers (14 to 17 years) will engage in unsafe or dangerous activities, get into trouble, or be harmed by someone else. The children echoed these fears. Thirty-two percent (32%) of African American and 40 percent of Hispanic children reported that they were worried greatly that someone on drugs might hurt them. These proportions compared to only 12 percent for white children. Approximately 14 percent of Black and 30 percent of Hispanic children and teenagers compared to just 5 percent of white children reported that they worried a lot that they would be sexually

3

abused or raped. To some extent, the higher levels of fear and anxiety among these children and their parents may be reflective of their disproportionately large numbers living in poverty.[5] In point of fact, they are at higher risk for having these experiences.

While African Americans, in general, must brace themselves and be vigilant, African American men appear to have even more reason to look over their shoulders. While many of the same forces are operative against African American women, it appears that there is a concerted effort to derail African American men, in particular. The male-drain in the African American community is particularly acute with little prospect of relief, given the high incidence of crime and homicide. African American males are continuing to be incarcerated en masse daily around the country.

African American men comprise a disproportionate share of the inmate population in United States prisons and jails. Even though they are roughly 6 percent of the total United States population, they represented 28 percent of the federal inmates and 48 percent of state inmates in 1990.[6] That same year, their rate of incarceration in the United States (3,109 per 100,000) far exceeded that of South Africa (729 per 100,000).[7] Andrew Hacker notes that while the proportion of white Americans in prison over the past 60 years has decreased, that of African Americans behind bars has increased dramatically.[8] For example, in 1930, the United States inmate population was 76.7 percent white and only 22.4 percent African American; by 1986, the percent of white Americans in prison had decreased to 39.6 percent, while the percent of incarcerated African Americans had increased to 45.3 percent.[9] Hacker analyzes the shift within the context of his broader examination of racism as a barrier to economic mobility.

A recent report issued by the National Center for Institutions and Alternatives examines the rise in drug arrests and its impact on African Americans in the city of Baltimore.[10] According to this report, while drug use among white Americans, African Americans, and Hispanic Americans is proportional to the population of each group, African Americans are disproportionately targeted. For example, African Americans were five times more likely than whites to be arrested for drug offenses in Baltimore in 1991. Thus, such policy choices contributed to making African Americans, who comprise 60 percent of Baltimore's population, represent 78 percent of arrests in Baltimore in 1991.[11] Moreover, 91 percent of juvenile drug arrests in Baltimore were African American youth, compared to 9 percent of white American youth. According to the report, "an African American youth was 100 times more likely to be charged with the sale of drugs in Baltimore than a white youth."[12] While this report is based on Baltimore, Maryland, it is probably safe to surmise that similar numbers hold true for most major urban areas where the economic and social conditions are similar.

The word is out in many quarters that the African American male is an endangered species.[13] This notion is supported by facts such as the high proportion of African American males incarcerated or involved in some aspect of the criminal justice system, the high homicidal rate, the astronomical rise and spread of the AIDS virus, and the continuing growth of drug abuse and its associated violence, particularly among our young. Added to these, is the under-education and miseducation of our youth, low teacher expectations, tracking in schools, placement in special education classes, truancy, expulsion, and ultimately, school drop out.

If we are to save the African American family and do our part to ensure its survival into the next century and beyond, we must begin to look at the structural and environmental conditions that give rise to the negative conditions that so many African Americans face. As we examine them, we must develop strategies and means for implementing change at all levels—structurally, environmentally and individually.

More intensive and more comprehensive programs at the federal, state and local community level are direly needed. In order for severely disadvantaged populations to benefit equally with other populations, they need to have access to a greater amount and more adequate services. A wide range of social and economic interventions, along with concerted efforts by governmental and community and civic organizations, must be undertaken to improve conditions of African Americans. In addition, educational and social support programs could bring about attitudinal and behavioral changes in children and adults, and empower parents in high risk environments. The costs involved in implementing corrective measures is insignificant compared to future costs to the nation if national public policy continues to be guided by lethargy and inaction.

Recognizing that African American men are but one, albeit, critical link in the African American family, this volume focuses on African American males.

The chapters address some of these pressing issues affecting African American men. In the chapter, "Reaffirming Young African Males: Mentoring and Community Involvement by Fraternities and Other Groups," Dionne J. Jones, Victor E. Bibbins, and Ronald Henderson assess mentoring as a strategy for reaffirming young African American males and guiding them toward positive achievement. While the authors emphasize that mentoring in itself is not a solution to the multiple problems that African American male youth face, they envision it as one component of a multi-faceted approach designed to improve the life chances of African American youth. Through structured mentoring relationships, an older, established, and successful figure can serve as a positive role model to an at-risk youth and can offer that youth guidance, support, encouragement, and even access to a given career path.

The next chapter, "Health Status of African American Men" by Lawrence E. Gary, assesses the current health status of African American males. Drawing on national data, Gary illustrates that African American males fare poorly when compared to their white counterparts on a wide range of health indicators. This is indicated by morality and morbidity rates, cancer rates, and the frequency of use of health services. Gary recommends that social policy be designed to remedy the conditions that place African Americans at health risk and to encourage positive behaviors.

Victor De La Cancela takes a fresh look at "coolin" among African American and Latino men by exploring the connections between "male posturing" among these two ethnically distinct groups. In his article "'Coolin': The Psychosocial Communication of African and Latino Men," he argues that, contrary to widespread belief, masculine postures signify more than destructive acts of rebellion. De La Cancela illustrates that an understanding of the true significance of "coolin" has important implications for positive interventions in African American and Latino male communities. This speaks to the importance of culturally contextualizing often misunderstood behaviors by these ethnic groups.

Gayle D. Weaver and Lawrence E. Gary's chapter, "Stressful Life Event, Psychosocial Resources, and Depressive Symptoms Among Older African American Men," addresses the mental health of elderly African American men. In a study focusing on this often neglected segment of the African American population, Weaver and Gary examine the correlation between depressive symptoms and a variety of social, economic, and demographic factors. They conclude that household income, experience of stressful life events, and self-perceptions of health are factors that impact depression among elderly African American men. Weaver and Gary also stress the need for further research in a field which all too often treats elderly African Americans as a homogenous group.

In "The Gender Role and Contraceptive Attitudes of Young Men: Implications for Future African American Families," Bruce H. Wade explores the subject of contraceptive attitudes among young African American males. Through a study of 60 African American youth in Atlanta, Georgia, Wade's findings indicate that half of the youth surveyed received inadequate information about contraception to be the female's responsibility. In light of such findings, Wade urges that increased emphasis should be placed on the education of both parents and youth on contraceptive issues.

Ronald K. Barrett analyzes a number of theoretical models which have been used to explain violence among urban youth in "Urban Adolescent Homicidal Violence: An Emerging Public Health Concern." Barrett addresses the shortcomings of these theoretical frameworks pointing to the inadequacies in the assumptions made by some of the models. He acknowledges the value of each theory noting that each can provide insight into the complex phenomenon of urban adolescent homicidal violence.

Turning to the psychological and spiritual development of African American males, Edward P. Wimberly's article, "Pastoral Counseling with African American Men," presents an approach to pastoral counseling geared toward enabling African American men to tap their inner sources of strength. Wimberly examines the destructive narratives on which African American men base their lives and offers a provocative analysis of their cultural and spiritual resources available to them for rewriting those narratives. These men can draw, for example, on the African American heritage of equalitarian relationships and androgynous roles as they work to replace destructive, oppressing narratives with positive, enabling ones.

Phylis Johnson and Thomas A. Birk explore the role of African American radio stations in promoting positive behaviors within the African American male community in their chapter "The Role of African American-Owned Radio in Health Promotion: Community Service Projects Targeting Young African American Males." Their survey of African American radio stations reveals that the majority of these stations are engaged in public service promotional activity on an ongoing basis. These activities included drug awareness campaigns, health-related messages, promotion of non-violent behavior, and voter registration drives. The authors propose that radio, as a medium which reaches a large audience and which has the potential to forge partnerships among its listeners, can be a source of positive change in the African American community.

As the authors in this volume attest, African American males are a precious resource. As such, they must be nurtured during childhood and throughout the life cycle.

NOTES

1. Robert Hill, *Strengths of Black Families* (Washington, DC: National Urban League, 1972).

2. U.S. Department of Commerce, Bureau of the Census, *Statistical Abstract of the United States 1992* (Washington, DC: Government Printing Office, 1992), p. 449.

3. *Quarterly Economic Report of the African American Worker* 4th Quarter, Monica B. Kuumba (ed.) (Washington, DC: National Urban League Research Department, 1992).

4. National Commission on Children, *Speaking of Kids: A National Survey of Children and Parents* (Washington, DC: Author, 1991).

5. Ibid.

6. James Stephan, *Census of State and Federal Correctional Facilities, 1990*, U.S. Department of Justice, NCJ-137003 (Washington, DC: Government Printing Office, May 1992).

7. Marc Mauer, *Americans Behind Bars: A Comparison of International Rates of Incarceration* (Washington, DC: The Sentencing Project, January 1991), p.5.

8. Andrew Hacker, *Two Nations: Black and White, Separate, Hostile, Unequal* (New York: Charles Scribner's Sons, 1992).

9. Ibid., p. 196.

10. National Center for Institutions and Alternatives, *Hobbling a Generation* (Washington, DC: Author, 1991).

11. Ibid., 5.

12. Ibid.

13. Jewelle Taylor Gibbs, "Black Adolescents and Youth: An Update on Endangered Species," In Reginald L. Jones (ed.), *Black Adolescents* (Berkeley, CA: Cobbs & Henry Publishers, 1989), 3–27.

Reaffirming Young African American Males: Mentoring and Community Involvement By Fraternities and Other Groups

Dionne J. Jones, Victor E. Bibbins and Ronald D. Henderson

Myriad problems beset the African American community, particularly our youth. The high school dropout rate is unacceptably high, as is teenage pregnancy. The AIDS epidemic ravages our community, disproportionately afflicting our children, and homicide appears to be an everyday occurrence for many of our youth. Far too many of our young men have easy access to drugs and weapons, making violence a way of life for many. The research literature suggests that when youth are engaged in meaningful activities with caring adults, they can and do succeed. This study assesses several mentoring programs—mentors and mentees—to obtain their perceptions of the effectiveness of their involvement. Both mentors and mentees report that their participation has been valuable.

Growing up in a hostile world and bombarded with negative images and stereotypes of self, many young African American males find themselves trapped in a cycle of despair. Many succumb to the unrelenting pressures of their external environment. At a time when our country's educational system is failing to provide adequate education for young African Americans, and high unemployment prevails in the African American community with even higher rates among its youth, when an epidemic of drugs sweeps the African American community and engulfs its young, and with AIDS becoming more rampant, we must create means to save our youth. One way to achieve this is to dislodge them from a fast track to self-destruction by reaffirming them to regain a wholesome sense of self.

The problems facing young African Americans today are both external and internal. Internally, many experience low self-esteem, lacking the vision for a hopeful future. Externally, poverty and negative environmental conditions deprive many African American children of wholesome development.

In 1990, African Americans represented 15.0 percent of the total United States population 19 years old and under.[1] More importantly, they represented more than one third of the total African American population. Interestingly, the proportion of males exceeded the proportion of females in the younger age groups.[2]

In 1991, just over one-third (35.9%) of all African American children under 18 years lived with two parents while more than one half (57.5%) lived with one parent. Moreover, more than two-thirds of these children who lived in female-headed households subsisted in poverty.[3] The death rate per 100,000 males ages 10 to 14 years is 44.3 compared to 27.6 for their female counterparts; in the 15 to 19 year age group, the rate is 76.2 for males and 48.6 for females.[4] The official Department of Labor unemployment rate for teenaged African American males was 36.5% in 1991, slightly above the rate for African American female teenagers (36.1%). The National Urban League's Hidden Unemployment Index reports a rate of 56.9 prcent for both males and females.[5]

Notwithstanding, some African American males are succeeding against the odds. Thirty-two percent (32%) of them graduating from high school enrolled in college in 1991 compared to 31.4 percent of African American females, 41.9 percent of white males, and 42.1 of white females.[6] These statistics support the view held by many that given the right conditions and resources, African American youth can succeed.

The purpose of this article is to highlight the findings of a study that examined the efforts of several major African American fraternities and organizations which are actively working with African American youth to enhance their life conditions. Some of these groups target African American youth in general, but others gear their programming efforts toward males only. While recognizing that the vast problems existing in the African American community pervade across gender and class lines, this article focuses only on an assessment of programs involving African American males.

The study addresses the following research questions:

1.   What is the profile of the men who volunteer to work with youth in these organizations?

2.   What is the profile of the youth who participate in mentoring programs?

3.   What are the volunteers' perceptions of their success in working with African American youth?

4.   What are some of the barriers to success as perceived by the volunteers?

UTILITY OF MENTORING PROGRAMS

It has been argued vociferously that African American adolescents and youth, particularly males, in contemporary American society are becoming an endangered species. Ostensively, many well meaning professionals, including scores of African Americans, perceive these youth as wasted human resources. Numerous educators have simply written them off as uneducable; the juvenile justice system has failed to rehabilitate them; our mental health programs have ignored and/or excluded them repeatedly; and social welfare institutions appear inadequate in responding to the multi-complex nature of their problems.[7]

If this situation is a conclusive pronouncement of the future plight of African American youth, then we are, indeed, facing a devastating infirmity in the psychosocial-economic fabric of our society. Conversely, a concerted stream of conscious optimism has emerged from this dismal reality. Thus, the loud alarms sounding on this issue for more than a decade have invoked a number of intervening therapeutic responses.

Just as one's eyes may experience pain when forced to adjust to a lighted room, the gatekeepers of the African American community were so illuminated to the painful reality that they had neglected to achieve the kind of educational, cultural, economic, emotional, moral, political, and social supports required to meet the needs of our emerging youth. This reaction stimulated a poignant cry within the African American community which, in turn, generated renewed thinking and commitment for positive action. Rather than allow ourselves to be defeated by our own admission, this undesirable reality prompted us to motivate and mobilize ourselves as effective agents of change.

One programmatic initiative implemented to heal the more than obvious wounds of African American male youth is the increased utilization of various kinds of mentoring programs from private, non-profit, fraternal, civic, and church organizations. To a large extent, these activities were initiated in response to poor economic conditions which produced inadequacies in effective education, employment, family and social services, delinquency- prevention counseling, and other public programs.

Master and apprentice, teacher and student, physician and intern are all familiar pairings. They all involve a basic relationship in which an older, more experienced person (MENTOR) takes a younger, less knowledgeable person (MENTEE) under his or her wing.[8] This long standing practice of mentoring represents one of the most inclusive and salient responses to solving the problems of African American male youth. Regardless of the specific nature and/or structure of mentoring activities (career enrichment, preventive, remedial, tutorial), they seem to have an enormous influence in shaping behavior. Modeling has been known to play a major role in educational and psychosocial development. Thus, getting African American male youth to identify with [a] positive individual[s] can lead them to incorporate that positiveness into their own identity.[9]

Over the past decade, there has been a deliberate, systematic and tenacious resurgence of mentoring as a strategy to help solve the problems facing African American male youth. The precise impact of these interventions are not yet known. It is reasonable to deduce, however, that there are numerous rewards for both mentors and mentees.[10] While mentoring alone will not solve all the myriad problems that African American male youth face, it may, indeed, represent an integral part of the solution and may have the potential to stop the problems from hemorrhaging.

There are various types of mentoring programs. Some, like The Black Achievers Program which began in 1971 at the Harlem YMCA, encourage the educational and career development of disadvantaged youth. This program uses African American professionals as mentors for at-risk youth. The mentors, who are nominated and financed by their companies, commit 40 hours a year to activities such as sharing their career path with students, participating in career fairs, having students spend a day at their workplace, helping students with college applications, raising money for scholarships, and offering general support and encouragement. This program has been replicated in 40 cities and 32 others are developing similar models.[11]

Another highly successful mentoring program is Career Beginnings which is based at the Center for Corporate and Education Initiatives at Brandeis University. While Career Beginnings is multifaceted, one key aspect of the program is mentoring. At-risk high school students, likely to succeed in college, are chosen to participate and are matched with mentors who are successful, working professionals. These students are from disadvantaged backgrounds, a majority of whom are minorities: 65 percent are African American, 18 percent are Hispanic, and 8 percent are Asian. More than 2,000 students per year have been served by this program in 21 cities and 13 states. Of the 10,000 students finishing the program, 95 percent have completed high school and over 65 percent have progressed to college.[12]

At Southern Illinois University, the mentoring program offers an example of how colleges can help students who are ill-prepared for college life. The program targets first term "special admissions students" who did not meet the criteria of high school rank and admissions test scores, but were admitted on the basis of academic potential. Like Career Beginnings, the program is multifaceted, but utilizes mentoring as an important component. Retired faculty serve as mentors, offering experience and guidance. Feedback from students suggest that mentoring has proven valuable.[13]

Other mentoring programs aim at discouraging crime among at- risk youth. For example, the San Antonio Independent School District collaborated with the Department of Safety to establish a comprehensive school-based prevention program. The intervention officers became involved in students' personal and academic lives and provided mentoring, counseling, and teaching. Thus, the officers served as role models and mentors for the youth, helping to reinforce the importance of working hard, staying in school, and more importantly, helping to maintain a bond between the children and adults.[14]

SURVEY OF FRATERNITIES AND COMMUNITY ORGANIZATIONS

This is an exploratory, descriptive study which utilized a multi-level design. At the first level, a convenience sample of organizations was selected. At the second level, individuals from the various organizations engaged in mentoring activities were targeted as the unit of analysis. Youth in the programs were targeted at the third level.

METHOD

Sample

The fraternities and organizations involved are: Alpha Phi Alpha, Kappa Alpha Psi, Omega Psi Phi, Concerned Black Men, The Institute for Academic and Social Development, and the D.C. National Guard. Table 1 gives a breakdown of the first level of the sample. A brief historical profile of the community involvement efforts of these organizations is presented to provide a frame of reference.

African American fraternities began during the early part of the Twentieth Century. Contrary to conventional wisdom, not all of the prominent African American Greek-letter societies were founded at Historically Black Colleges and Universities. For example, Alpha Phi Alpha was founded at Cornell University in 1906.[15] Similarly, Kappa Alpha Psi was founded at Indiana University in 1911.[16] Omega Psi Phi, however, was founded at Howard University also in 1911.[17] These organizations began for a variety of reasons—cultural, psychological, social, and intellectual—based on the campus setting. The community and campus environments during the early years of these organizations were crucial factors in the evolution of their structure and functions. Moreover, as the men began to graduate and form alumni groups, community service emerged as an important role. The respondents in the sample were in the graduate chapters of the fraternities.

African American male Greek-letter societies have a vast array of activities that provide support to the African American community. The following list is suggestive of the wide range of community endeavors: mentoring, tutoring, scholarship programs, teenage pregnancy prevention programs, youth clubs, career fairs, adopt-a-school, sponsoring athletic teams, literary/talent contests, voter registration drives, support of Africare and civil rights organizations, and so forth.

TABLE 1
Breakdown of the Sample

Organization	No. of Mentors	%
Total	51	100.0
Alpha Phi Alpha	8	15.7
Kappa Alpha Psi	10	19.6
Omega Psi Phi	10	19.6
Concerned Black Men	2	3.9
Institute for Academic & Social Development	11	21.6
D.C. National Guard	10	19.6

The range and depth of programs vary for the fraternities. In some instances, the activity is solely the creation and responsibility of the fraternity. In other cases, the endeavor is supplemental to existing services provided by schools and other agencies or organizations.

The Washington, D.C. Chapter of Concerned Black Men, Inc., was founded in 1982 as a nonprofit organization of male volunteers. Its purpose is to provide positive, male role models and build stronger channels of communication between adults and children. With its motto, "Caring for Our Youth," Concerned Black Men sponsors a variety of programs and activities promoting educational, cultural and social development. It works with D.C. public schools and a number of community organizations and agencies.[18]

The Institute for Academic and Social Development was founded in 1989 as an independent, nonprofit organization. Its primary purpose is to promote academic achievement and social development among educationally discouraged and troubled youth. The Institute's activities include a broad range of academic enrichment, social development, and public awareness initiatives.[19]

The D.C. National Guard is a local branch of the U.S. Armed Forces. One of its missions includes providing community service in the Washington, D.C. area. It began these activities with a Youth Leadership Camp during the 1970s involving youth in discussion groups with speakers, sports and team competition, and a graduation ceremony. Recruitment for the youth took place in the schools.

As can be seen, the latter three organizations engage in activities very similar to the fraternities mentioned above.

Fifty-four youth from two of the six organizations also participated in the study.

Instrument

A self-administered survey was developed for fraternity brothers and other males in community organizations engaged in mentoring, tutoring and other enrichment services with African American youth. The survey asked for demographic information about the mentors to obtain a profile of them. It also requested information regarding the services and activities engaged in by the respondents as well as their perceptions of their effectiveness with the youth.

A self-administered survey was also developed for youth who are recipients of services in the programs. In addition to obtaining demographic information, the survey sought to obtain views of the youth on the usefulness of the program to them, as well as on their plans to continue in the program.

Data Collection Procedures

Some of the mentor surveys were administered in person during scheduled group meetings, while others were mailed to the program coordinators for distribution at group meetings. The surveys completed by youth were also administered during scheduled meetings. Both mentor and youth surveys took approximately 10 minutes to complete.

Findings

Profile of Volunteers. The male volunteers ranged in ages from under 25 to over 60 years. The majority (47.1%) was in the 26 to 35 years age range. The next highest proportion (19.6%) was in the 36 to 45 years age range, followed by the 46 to 55 years age range (13.7%). Their marital status is as follows: one-third (33%) are single, 41.2 percent are married, and the remainder are either separated or divorced. More than half (52.9%) have no children living at home with them. Almost one-quarter (23.5%) have one child living at home and 9.8 percent of the sample have two children living at home with them.

The overwhelming majority of the sample (76.5%) had earned a bachelor's degree or higher. Commensurate with their education, 80 percent of respondents had an annual salary greater than $31,000. As may be expected, then, most of the men perceived themselves to be either middle class (49.0%) or upper middle class (17.6%). The remaining one-third saw themselves as lower middle class (13.7%) or working class (19.6%). Contrary to expectation, more than one-quarter of the men (28.9%) perceived their socioeconomic status while growing up to be middle class, while 20 percent of them perceived themselves as lower middle class and 40 percent as working class. Moreover, more than one-half of the respondents (51.0%) grew up with both parents. One-quarter of them (25.5%) grew up with one parent. The remainder grew up with a grandparent or a combination of relatives (see Table 2).

The *one* significant individual who impacted most on the lives of these men was a member of the family, typically mother (41.2%) or father (21.9%). Grandparents, brothers, sisters, and teachers were also identified as significant influences. Another question asked the respondents to identify other significant individuals in their lives while they were growing up. Here again, parents were given greatest credit. Responses were as follows: parents (29.2%), teachers (22.9%), and a combination of others (27.1%). The majority of the respondents scored high on a scale of spiritual development which included belief in a Supreme Being, regular church attendance, prayer and meditation, and belief in fate/destiny and the hereafter. Out of a possible maximum score of 30, the mean score for the group was 23.5.

TABLE 2
Socio-Demographic Characteristics of Mentors—A Profile
(N=51)

Characteristics	N	%
Age		
Under 25 years	5	9.8
26–35 years	24	47.1
36–45 years	10	19.6
46–55 years	7	13.7
56–60 years	2	3.9
Over 60 years	3	5.9
Education		
High School	3	5.9
Some College	9	17.6
Bachelor's Degree	20	39.2
Master's Degree	14	27.5
Doctorate Degree	4	7.8
Professional Degree	1	2.0
Income*		
Under $30,000	10	20.0
$30–$40,999	16	32.0
$41–$50,999	12	24.0
$51–$60,999	1	2.0
$61–$70,000	5	9.8
$71,000+	6	11.8
Marital Status*		
Single	17	33.3
Married	21	41.2
Separated/Divorced	7	13.7
Current Socioeconomic Status		
Upper Middle Class	9	17.7
Middle Class	25	49.0
Lower Middle Class	7	13.7
Working Class	10	19.6
Socioeconomic Status While Growing Up*		
Upper Middle Class	5	11.1
Middle Class	13	28.9
Lower Middle Class	9	20.0
Working Class	18	40.0
Primarily Grew Up With		
One Parent	13	25.5
Both Parents	26	51.0
Grandparents	4	7.8
Other	3	5.9
Combination	5	9.8

* Totals do not add to 100% due to missing data.

Profile of Youth. Most of the youth were between the ages of 10 to 21 years. The majority (72.2%) was in the 14 to 17 years age range; 22.2 percent were between 10 to 13 years. Most of the students were in junior high school (70.4%); 29.6 percent were in high school. More than half of the youth reported that they were living with one parent (51.9%). Almost one-third of them (31.5%) were living with both parents, however. The majority of them had siblings; 61.1 percent had one to two brothers or sisters and 16.7 percent had three to five brothers or sisters (see Table 3).

Involvement with their particular program ranged from one month to more than one year for the youth, with most being involved for more than three months. These program participants overwhelmingly (84.9%) indicated that the services had helped them. A large proportion of them (64.8%) cited their reasons for participating in the programs was to "learn something." The services received most often by the youth were: Mentoring (62.3%), counseling (15.1%), and tutoring (11.3%). Specific areas in which the students feel that they have been helped are: setting goals for the future (50.0%), helping them stay away from drugs and alcohol (48.1%), feeling good about their future (40.4%), feeling better about themselves (38.5%), improvement in grades (30.8%), and making career choices (28.8%). Areas in which mentees continue to need help are: math and science (64.7%), getting part time jobs (51.0%), staying out of trouble (31.4%), and reading (21.6%). The majority of the youth (69.2%) planned to continue in the program, while 28.8 percent were undecided, and 1.9 percent or one student did not plan to continue.

Impact of the Programs. A number of reasons were cited by the mentors for their involvement in community work. Most (30.8%) felt they "could make a difference," (20.5%) felt they wanted to "give back to the community." The others (46.1%) gave a combination of reasons. The overwhelming majority of respondents (62.5%) indicated that they were involved in a variety of activities with youth, which included tutoring, mentoring, and counseling. Some of the mentoring activities engaged in by the mentors were: coaching, holding discussion groups, developing life skills, classroom activities, passing the torch, guide right, and field trips. Over one-half (56.3%) of them met once a week with the youth; 15.6 percent met twice a week and another 15.6 percent met twice a month. The remaining 12.5 percent either met at other times or did not respond to the questions.

Almost half (49%) of the mentors perceived that the youth had a positive attitude towards life. Possibly due to such positive attitudes among the youth, the mentors felt that their efforts had a positive influence on them (62.8%), served as a deterrent to crime among the youth (68.9%), and generally improved the quality of life for mentees (64.5%). Comments from mentors about the impact of their work with youth include: "Providing them with direction," "giving them the courage with the push to do anything they set their minds to do," "molding young Black males to become well-rounded productive citizens," "encouraging them to continue their education," "at the very least raised the level of awareness concerning themselves and their actions," "realistic alternatives to crime because I used to be like them," "role model, builder of self-esteem," "raised their self-confidence," and "improvement in academics." No doubt, due to their positive feelings about the program, more than three-quarters (77.8%) of the mentors plan to continue their community involvement with youth. The remaining respondents were undecided about continuing.

TABLE 3
Selected Characteristics of the Youth—A Profile
(N=54)

Characteristics	N	%
Age		
10–13 years	12	22.2
14–17 years	39	72.2
18–21 years	3	5.6
Education		
Junior High School	38	70.4
High School	16	29.6
Family		
One Parent	28	51.9
Both Parents	17	31.5
Grandparents	6	11.1
Other	3	5.6
Siblings		
None	10	18.5
1 to 2	33	61.1
3 to 5	9	16.7
More than 5	2	3.7
Length of time involved with program		
Less than 1 month	6	11.1
1–3 months	12	22.2
3–6 months	17	31.5
6–12 months	7	13.0
More than 1 year	12	22.2
Reason for attending program		
Can learn something	35	64.8
Something to do	12	22.2
Authorities make me	2	3.7
Parents make me	1	1.9
Other	4	7.5

Barriers to Success. The findings, for the most part, indicate that both the mentors and mentees feel positive about the programs and activities. The mentors, however, have concern about some areas which they see as barriers to success among the mentees. Areas causing the greatest concern were the youths' attitudes, attention span, and lack of obedience. Poor self-esteem and discipline in the home were also problems faced by the mentors. Comments by the mentors include: "little or no family involvement or support," "earning their trust," "dysfunctional homes—single mothers, drugs, alcohol, violence," "influences by other youth with negative views," "getting enough volunteers to come out to work with the kids," "the kids are disrespectful, rude, have no fear of authority," and "self-destructive mentality, identifying too strongly with messages from the entertainment industry."

Conclusion

This was an exploratory study whose sample size does not lend itself to generalizations about all mentoring programs. Further, mentees from all the groups did not participate. However, some of the findings of this study confirm those of previous studies. For example, mentoring appears to be a part of the solution to the problems plaguing urban communities. Both the mentors and mentees in this study reported that their participation in the programs was a useful exercise of their time.

The majority of the mentors are middle class, well educated with bachelor's and master's degrees, and between the ages of 26 to 45 years. Twice as many of them grew up in two-parent homes as did in single-parent homes. This is almost the reverse for the youth, 51 percent of whom are living in one-parent households.

In general, the mentors believe that the trend of violence and drug involvement among African American youth could be curbed with the involvement of positive and concerned parents as well as peers and role models. A strong family was seen as pivotal to aiding youth in developing positive attitudes. Additionally, the mentors felt that more programs are needed as well as more concerned parents and community residents to volunteer their time. Comments include: "they need to have an appreciation for life and self-worth," "sincere effort by government to curb the supply of illegal substances," "a realistic economic structure created for them to fit into and develop within," "give them realistic goals to achieve," "more Black male mentors willing to commit themselves and their time," "strong fathers and more religion in their lives," "family values reinstated," and "educate parents, more extracurricular activities for the youth, publicize more male/female role models."

IMPLICATIONS AND RECOMMENDATIONS

The findings of this study support previous research showing positive results for both mentors and mentees. However, it is not the authors' intention to suggest that mentoring is a panacea. Mentoring and after school tutoring and enrichment programs cannot and should not be substitutes for sound educational programs. At a more fundamental level, mentoring cannot always compensate for or overcome the powerful influences in the mentees' immediate environment.[20]

It is acknowledged, however, that mentoring does improve the social chances of disadvantaged youth by providing resources and important psychosocial support, as well as helping to solve the contradictions involved in entering the mainstream. Indeed, mentoring should be seen as only one component of a multi-faceted intervention program. It is not a solution in itself.

The African American community as a whole must become involved in the effort to save our youth. One important step is to join forces with school systems which must be held accountable at every level. Parents must work with teachers to let them know that they are interested in their children's educational process and welfare. In this way, the teachers will also be held accountable. Schools must understand the needs of their culturally diverse student populations. Teachers must be trained in useful and effective strategies for helping African American children and other cultural/ethnic group children become successful in the school process.

To be sure, many individuals and groups are involved in attempting this herculean task; however, there are hundreds of thousands of African American children, male and female, who must be served. To serve them and to reach them all, greater efforts and resources are needed. In particular, more male and female role models are needed for young African American children to emulate.

NOTES

1. U.S. Department of Commerce, Bureau of the Census, "Poverty in the United States, 1991," *Current Population Reports*, (Series P-60, No. 181), Table 5, pp. 10-15.

2. Billy Tidwell, Monica B. Kuumba, Dionne J. Jones, Betty Watson, "Fast Facts," *State of Black America 1993* (New York: National Urban League, 1993), 253.

3. Ibid., 254.

4. Ibid., 257.

5. Ibid., 259.

6. Ibid., 258.

7. Jewelle Taylor Gibbs, "Black Adolescents and Youth : An Update On Endangered Species," In Reginald L. Jones (ed.), *Black Adolescents* (Berkeley, CA: Cobbs & Henry Publishers, 1989), 3-27.

8. Robert A. Baron, *Behaviors in Organizations: Understanding and Managing the Human Side of Work*. Second Edition (Boston, MA: Allyn and Bacon, Inc., 1986), 56.

9. Ronald L. Taylor, "Psychosocial Development and Socialization," In Reginald L. Jones (ed.), *Black Adolescents* (Berkeley, CA: Cobbs & Henry Publishers, 1989), 155-174.

10. Baron, *Behaviors in Organizations*, 56.

11. Cheryl McCortie, "Mentoring Young Achievers," *Black Enterprise* 21 (June, 1991): 336-8.

12. Laura Stanley, "Mentoring: What Works—What Doesn't" *Across the Board* 28 (April, 1991): 55-6.

13. Douglas Bedient, Vivian Snyder and Mary Snyder, "Retirees Mentoring At-risk College Students," *Phi Delta Kappan* 73 (February, 1992): 462-3.

14. Joan H. Murphy, "Reading, Writing, and Intervention," *Security Management* 36 (August 1992): 26-30.

15. Charles Wesley, *The History of Alpha Phi Alpha* (Washington, DC: Association for the Study of Negro Life and History, 1935).

16. William L. Crump, *The Story of Kappa Alpha Psi: A History of the Beginning and Development of a College Greek Letter Organization 1911–1991*. Fourth Edition.

17. Robert Lewis Gill, *The Omega Psi Phi Fraternity and the Men Who Made Its History* (Washington, DC: Omega Psi Phi, 1940).

18. Concerned Black Men, Inc., "Caring for Our Youth." A Pamphlet. (Washington, DC: Author).

19. Institute for Academic and Social Development, Inc., A Pamphlet. (Forestville, MD: Author).

20. Erwin Flaxman, Carol Ascher, Charles Harrington, "Youth Mentoring: Programs and Practices," Urban Diversity Series No. 97, (1988).

Health Status of African American Men

Lawrence E. Gary

The health condition of African American men has emerged as a major policy issue confronting our society. Data from the National Center for Health Statistics were examined to determine the health status of African American men. African American men have higher mortality and morbidity rates than white males and they use health services less often than white males, with the exception of public mental health facilities. To correct these conditions, social policies should target the health-risk behaviors of African American men, as well as the industries which promote unhealthy life styles. The family is very important for health promotion, and research is needed in this area, especially from the perspective of African American men.

A number of writers have documented the crisis facing African American men.[1] An important aspect of this crisis is the health status of African American men. Recent years have witnessed a growing concern regarding the current health status of African American men. The fact that male fetuses are more likely to spontaneously abort than female fetuses sets the stage for the future health of African American male youth.[2] Some writers suggest that if African American men survive high infant mortality rates, low birth weight, the lack of preventive health care, and the recent threat of AIDS, they are still more likely than any other racial group to die before the age of 20.[3] More importantly, if health problems such as poor nutrition are neglected in early childhood, they are more likely to develop into serious diseases or disabilities later on. These facts alone indicate that African American men represent a very vulnerable group from a health perspective.

This article discusses national trends in the health status of African American men and makes comparisons with their white counterparts. Health status is measured here primarily in terms of mortality, morbidity, the use of health services, and a self-assessment of health status. Policy implications are made of the health status of African American men from the perspective of health-risk behavior or life styles and the importance of the family in health promotion.

HEALTH STATUS—MORTALITY AND MORBIDITY

Life Expectancy Rates

African American men have high mortality rates in comparison to other groups in our society. Life expectancy at birth serves as an important indicator of the health status for a given demographic group in our society. In 1989, the life expectancy at birth was 75.3 years for all American.[4] This was the highest in United States history. However, there are some notable differences when life expectancy is examined by race and sex. For example, in 1989, African American men had the lowest life expectancy, 64.8 years, and white women had the highest life expectancy rate, 78.6.[5] The life expectancy rates for white men, 71.8 years, and African American women, 73.5 years, were comparable in 1989. These data show that on average white men lived seven years longer than did their African American counterparts in 1989.

From a historical perspective, the life expectancy gap between African American men and white men has narrowed only slightly over the years. For example, in 1950, white men lived 7.6 years longer than African American men; however, by 1980, the gap in their respective life expectancy rate remained 6.9 years and by 1989, white men lived seven years longer than African American men.[6] Since 1960, the life expectancy ratio of African American men to white men has remained roughly the same as indicated in Table 1. It is interesting to note that the life expectancy rate of 64.8 years for African American men in 1989 is less than the rate of 66.5 years for white men in 1950.

TABLE 1
Trends in Selected Mortality Indicators of African American and White Men

Year	Age-Adjusted Death Rate (per 1000 persons)			Life Expectancy at Birth		
	White	African American	African American- White-Ratio	White	African American	African American- White-Ratio
1960	9.2	12.5	1.36	67.4	61.1*	.91
1970	8.9	13.2	1.48	68.0	60.0	.88
1975	8.0	11.6	1.45	69.5	62.4	.90
1980	7.5	11.1	1.48	70.7	63.8	.90
1982	7.1	10.4	1.46	71.5	65.1	.91
1984	6.9	10.1	1.46	71.8	65.6	.91
1987	6.7	10.2	1.52	72.2	65.2	.90
1988	6.6	10.4	1.58	72.3	64.9	.90
1989	6.4	10.3	1.61	72.7	64.8	.89

* African Americans and others
Source: U.S. Bureau of the Census, *Statistical Abstract of the United States: 1992* (Washington, DC: U.S. Government Printing Office, 1992), 76, 78.

Death Rates

Similar to life expectancy, the death rate in a population serves as a rudimentary measure of health status. A decrease in the death rate provides a good means of assessing the extent of overall health improvement in a given population. Due to the significant difference in the median age between the African American and white male populations, presenting death rates without adjusting for the reality of an older white population masks the disparity in death rate. For example, without adjusting for age, the white male death rate (per 1000 population) in 1989 was 9.3, compared to 10.1 for African American men.

Adjusting for age, however, yields a more realistic comparison between the two groups. The age-adjusted death rate (per 1000 population) for African American men in 1989 was 10.3, compared to 6.4 for white men. Table 1 illustrates the trend of an increasing ratio between the groups despite an overall decline in male death rates since 1960. The death rate for African American men in 1989 is higher than the rate for white men in 1960.

African American men have higher death rates than their white counterparts throughout the life cycle, except in the oldest category, 85 years and older. Age has an impact on the death rates and the resulting differentials between the two groups. For example, in 1989 the death rate for African American male infants under one year of age was 19.9; however, it was less than half the rate (9.1) for white male infants.[8] For adults 25 to 44 years of age, the death rate for African American men is approximately two and one half times that for white men. Furthermore, a number of studies have shown the effects of marital status on mortality rates.[9] In an analysis of the impact of race, sex, and marital status on morality rates, Geerken and Gove concluded:

> The data support the view that marriage is slightly more advantageous for white men than for Black men, while being unmarried is slightly more disadvantageous for white men than for Black men.[10]

Studies have consistently shown that married people have lower mortality than those who have never been married. These findings have some relevance to the shifting marital patterns in the African American community. African American men are more likely than are white men not to get married, to get divorced, and to live alone. For example, in 1991, only 46.7 percent of African American men 18 years old and over were married compared to 65.8 percent of white men.[11] The divorce rate is also high for African American men. In 1991, it was 239 for African American men, but less than half the rate (117) for white men.

Cause of Death

Death rates provide only a limited assessment of health status in a population. Cause of death is another, although still incomplete, indicator of health. Since 1960, diseases of the heart have been the leading cause of death among African American men, despite a significant decline from 381.2 in 1960 to 272.6 in 1989.[12] White men have experienced similar declines; death rates due to heart diseases dropped from 375.4 in 1960 to 205.9 in 1989. The improvements related to the drop in heart diseases among African American men become almost insignificant compared to the increase in death rates due to cancer. For example, in 1960 the death rate due to cancer was 158.5, and by 1989 it was 230.6, representing a 45 percent increase during this period.[13]

Table 2 contains data on age-adjusted death rates by cause of death for African American and white men. As can be seen, African American men were more than twice as likely as white men to die from diabetes, nephritis or nephrotic syndrome, septicemia, and drug and alcohol-related causes. They were more than three times as likely to die from human immunodeficiency virus (AIDS) and more than seven times as likely to die from homicide. The gap in deaths from drug-related causes between the two groups has increased since 1980.[14] An examination in the leading causes of death in 1989 reveals that the three leading causes of death are similar for African American and white men; namely, disease of the heart, cancer, and accidents.[15] However, homicide, the fourth leading cause of death for African American men in 1989, was *not* a leading cause of death for white men. On the other hand, suicide, the seventh leading cause of death for white men, was *not* a leading cause of death for African American men. AIDS was the sixth leading cause of death for African American men, but was not a leading cause of death for white men.

When causes of death are examined by specific age groups, a different picture emerges. The most noticeable difference is that death among young men are due mostly to external, not biological or genetic factors.[16] In 1989, the homicide death rate (per 100,000) ranged from 114.8 to 112.6 for African American men between 15 to 34 years compared to a range of 46.2 to 30.2 for African American men between 45 and 64 years.[17] Although African American men have a lower suicide death rate than white men, the suicide rates for young African American men are similar to those of young white men. For example, in 1989 the suicide rates were 22.0 and 24.9 for African American and white men, respectively between the ages of 25 to 34 years.[18] Moreover, older white men are much more likely to commit suicide than are older African American men. For example, in 1989, the suicide rates for older white men were 35.1 for those 65 to 75 years; 55.3 for ages 75 to 84; and 71.9 for ages 85 years and older. The rates ranged from 15.4 to 22.2 for comparable groups of African American men.

TABLE 2
Male Age-Adjusted Death Rates for Selected Causes According to Race: 1989
(Per 100,000 Population)

Cause of Death	African American	White	African American- White Ratio
Diseases of heart	272.6	205.9	1.32
Cerebrovascular diseases	54.1	28.0	1.93
Malignant neoplasm	230.6	157.2	1.47
Chronic obstructive pulmonary diseases	24.9	26.8	.93
Pneumonia and influenza	27.9	16.9	1.65
Chronic liver disease and cirrhosis	20.5	11.9	1.72
Diabetes mellitus	22.6	11.0	2.05
Nephritis, nephrotic syndrome	13.9	4.7	2.97
Septicemia	11.2	4.1	2.73
Atherosclerosis	3.3	3.4	.97
Human immunodeficiency virus (AIDS)	40.3	13.1	3.08
Natural causes	887.4	567.4	1.56
Accidents	67.3	47.8	1.41
Suicide	12.5	19.6	.64
Homicide and legal intervention	61.5	8.1	7.59
Drug induced causes	11.4	4.8	2.38
Alcohol induced causes	26.8	9.8	2.73
External causes	144.7	76.8	1.88

Source: National Center for Health Statistics, *Health, United States, 1991* (Hyattsville, MD: Public Health Service, 1992), 158.

HEALTH STATUS—ACUTE AND CHRONIC CONDITIONS

Acute Conditions

In contrast to illness, death is a relatively straightforward means of measuring health status in a community. In general, illness can be quite subjective.[19] Thus, in discussing morbidity as a component of health status, the subjective element is recognized. According to Mechanic, "much of the illness for which patients seek help is difficult to classify . . . and interview data on sickness tend to represent the patients' subjective appraisals of feelings both of a bodily and psychological nature and of the impact they have on their functioning."[20]

In the National Health Interview Survey (NHIS), acute conditions are defined as "illnesses and injuries that ordinarily last less than three (3) months [and] . . . are serious enough to have had an impact on behavior."[21] Examples of acute conditions are intestinal virus, viral infections, respiratory conditions, injuries, and digestive system conditions. Data from the NHIS, 1985–1987, show that low-income African American men had a higher number of acute conditions than did their higher income counterparts with the exception of those between 45 to 64 years.[22] As shown in Table 3, African American men were much less likely than were white men to suffer from acute conditions and these findings hold true for virtually all comparable age group. For example, between 1985–1987 the average annual number of acute conditions per 100 persons per year was 126.9 for African American men, while it was 166.7 for white men. In explaining the surprising finding that African American men have a lower rate of acute conditions, a recent report by U.S. Department of Health and Human Services concluded:

> Although Blacks had more bed-disability days and work-loss days than whites, they reported fewer overall acute conditions. Bed-disability and work-loss days may be regarded as an indication of the severity of a reported acute condition. This suggests that Blacks are more likely to report proportionately more severe acute conditions. Another possible explanation is that Blacks may have higher disability levels associated with acute conditions; i.e., although fewer, the episodes of acute conditions reported by Blacks result in more protracted disabilities. Finally, the lower reported incidence of acute conditions by Blacks concomitant with more work loss and disability days suggests that Blacks may delay seeking medical care.[23]

Chronic Conditions

As shown in Table 2, the death rates for African American men are higher than white men for all but two conditions: arteriosclerosis and chronic obstructive pulmonary. One particular chronic condition that has plagued the African American community is high blood pressure. The latest NHIS data show that blood pressure (borderline or high) is a serious problem among African Americans. For example, overall, 48.5 percent of African American men between the ages of 20 and 74 had elevated blood pressure (systolic pressure at least 140 mmHg or diastolic pressure at least 90 mmHg), compared to 43.1 of white men in that age range.[24] There is a relationship between age and elevated blood pressure among African American men; only 22.2 percent of African American men between the ages of 20 to 24 suffer from this condition, compared to 71.8 percent between the ages of 55 to 64. African American men are less likely to have borderline high and high serum cholesterol level than are white men.[25] In the NHIS data between 1976–1980, the age-adjusted borderline high serum cholesterol rate was 31.9 for white men between the ages of 20 to 74, but only 27.5 for African American men in the same age group. On the other hand, African American men were more likely to be overweight (body mass index greater than or equal to 27.8 kilograms/meter) than were white men.[26]

Another condition which has a high incidence in the African American male community is cancer. For most types of cancer, African American men have higher incidence than do white men.[27] For leukemia, non-Hodgkin's lymphoma, and urinary bladder cancers, white men have higher incidence rates than do African American men. The overall age-adjusted cancer incidence rates were 524.4 (number of new cases per 100,000 population) for African American men compared to 444.4 for white men in 1989. For the two most common types of cancer among African American men, namely lung (and bronchus) and prostate cancer, the incidence rates were almost 50 percent higher than those for white men. Death rates (per 100,000 population) related to the prostate gland and respiratory disorders are much higher for African American men than for white men. For example, in 1989, the death rate for prostate cancer among African American men (30.9) more than doubled the rate for white men (14.5).[28] Once African American men develop cancer, they are less likely to survive the condition than are white men.[29] For example, the five-year relative cancer survival rates (that is, the ratio of the observed survival rate for the patient group to the expected survival rate for persons in the general population similar to the patient group with respect to age, sex, race and calendar year of observation) were 48.4 for white men, but only 33.4 for African American men between 1983 to 1988, a ratio of 1.50. In other words, white men are one and a half times more likely to survive a cancerous condition than are African American men. This is especially true for oral cavity and pharynx.

OTHER DISABLING CONDITIONS

Mental Disorders

Although there is disagreement over the definition and constitution of mental illness,[30] some data are available on admissions to mental health institutions for psychiatric services. The latest data show that nonwhite men are more than twice as likely as white men to be admitted to mental health institutions as inpatients. For example, in 1986, the inpatient admission rate (per 100,000 civilian population) was 706.1 for white men, and 1514.2 for nonwhite men.[31] Similar disproportionate rates exist for inpatient admissions to state and county mental hospitals and veteran's medical centers. In 1986, the inpatient admissions rate to state and county hospitals for nonwhite men was 419.7, but only 147.2 for white men, a ratio of 2.8 to 1. As shown in Table 3, once they are admitted to mental health facilities, African American men stay longer than white men.

Disability and Restricted Activity

Being ill or having a chronic or acute condition has a tremendous impact on one's ability to carry on certain activities such as working, going to school or participating in

TABLE 3
The Male Morbidity Rates for Selected Conditions According to Race

Conditions and Characteristics	African American	White
Average annual number of acute conditions, all ages	126.9	166.7
Average annual number of acute conditions, family income below $20,000	133.4	172.8
Average annual number of acute conditions, family income above $20,000	119.5	171.2
Average annual percent of persons with restricted limitation, all ages	13.6	13.5
Average annual percent of persons with restricted limitation, under 18 years	6.5	5.8
Average annual percent of persons with restricted limitation, 45–64 years	28.4	21.5
Average annual percent of persons with restricted limitation, family income less $20,000	17.7	21.0
Average annual percent of persons with restricted limitation, family income more $20,000	7.0	9.9
Elevated blood pressure among persons 20–74 years, 1976–1980	48.5	43.1
Elevated blood pressure among persons 35–44 years, 1976–1980	52.8	37.7
Elevated blood pressure among persons 55–64 years, 1976–1980	71.8	57.6
Hypertension among persons 20–74 years, 1976–1980	50.5	44.8
Percent of population with borderline high serum cholesterol, 1976–1980	27.5	31.9
Percent of population with high serum cholesterol, 1976–1980	25.7	26.0
Percent of population overweight for persons 20–74 years, 1976–1980	27.5	24.9
Percent of population overweight for persons 45–54 years, 1976–1980	41.4	30.5
Age-adjusted cancer incidence rates, 1989	524.4	444.4
Age-adjusted cancer incidence rates for prostate gland, 1989	142.0	108.5
Age-adjusted cancer incidence rates for lung and bronchus, 1989	118.3	78.9
Cancer survival rates for all sites, 1983–1988	33.4	48.4
Cancer survival rates for oral cavity and pharynx, 1983–1988	26.2	52.1
Cancer survival rates for prostate gland, 1983–1988	62.9	77.6
Inpatient admissions rates to all type of psychiatric services, 1986	1514.2*	706.1
Inpatient admissions rates to State and County hospitals, 1986	419.7*	147.2
Inpatient admissions rates to Veteran Medical Centers, 1986	269.1*	128.3
Median days of stay for persons in inpatient-psychiatric service, 1986	16.0	15.0
Outpatient admission rates to all type of psychiatric services, 1986	1031.5*	978.8
Percent of persons assessed their health poor or fair, 1985–1987	13.3	8.7
Percent of persons between 18–44 years assessed their health poor or fair, 1985–1987	9.1	4.3

* African Americans and Others
Source: Peter Ries, *Health of Black and White Americans*, 1985–1987 (Hyattsville, MD: National Center for Health Statistics, 1990), 25, 26, 45–50, 54–55; National Center for Health Statistics, *Health, United States, 1991* (Hyattsville, MD: Public Health Service, 1992), 198, 199, 210, 212–214; and Ronald W. Manderscheid and Mary A. Sonnenschein, eds., *Mental Health, United States, 1992*, Center for Mental Health and Institute for Mental Health (Washington, DC: U.S. Government Printing Office, 1992), 283–294.

community activities. Disability, restricted activity or limitation of activity have been used to measure the social and psychological impact of being ill or sick on a person. As shown in Table 3, illness tends to restrict the activities of African American men more than it does the activities of white men, although family income also has an impact.[33] According to NHIS data between 1985-1987, the average annual number of restricted-activity days per person due to acute or chronic conditions was 12.8 for white men and 14.2 for African American men. Controlling for income, however, a different pattern emerges. For instance, the average annual number of restricted-activity days was higher for white men (18.3) than for African American men (17.5) whose family income was less than $20,000.[34] The rates were similar for the two groups, however, when family income was more than $20,000.

Health Assessment and Use of Health Services

Assessment by respondents of their health and their use of health services are also useful indicators of health status. In 1990, white men were more likely to visit a physician than were African American men.[35] The interval since last contact with a physician was longer for African American men than their white male counterparts. In 1989, African American men were less likely to visit a dentist than were white men. Dental health, often ignored in the overall assessment of health status of African Americans, is both reflective and determinative of an individual's health. In general, there has been a long-term decline in both tooth loss and edentulism, complete toothlessness, within the United States population. As is well-known, edentulism increases with age. Among the 45 and over population, African Americans have higher rates of edentulism than whites, except in the 45 to 54 age group.[36] An analysis of the reasons given for visiting the dentist suggests that African American men are more concerned with serious dental problems, such as having teeth pulled, and are less concerned with regular preventive maintenance. A sizable proportion (38.4%) of African American men reported visiting the dentist in 1985 to have teeth extracted or surgery performed, compared to only 11.2 percent of white men.[37] By contrast, 38.4 percent of white men went to the dentist for regular check ups, compared to only 18.4 percent of African American men.

In assessing their health, African American men tended to rate their health as being poor or fair more often than white men.[38] The 1985-1987 NHIS data indicate that 13.3 percent of African American men rated their health as poor or fair compared to 8.7 percent of white men. Older African American men were also more likely than their younger counterparts to rate their health as poor or fair. Family income had an impact on how men rated their health. Both African American and white men were more likely to rate their health as poor or fair when their family income was less than $20,000 than when it was over $20,000.

CONCLUSIONS AND POLICY IMPLICATIONS

This analysis shows that the health status of African American men is poor compared to that of white men. Their poor health status suggests that a large number of African American men will be removed from their families through death or will become unable to work due to serious physical and psychological disabilities. The high morbidity and mortality rates of African American men have had devastating effects on their emotional health as well as on that of their families and friends. While it is true that the health care system has limited the access to medical care for African American men, their lifestyles may also be a contributing factor to their health problems. For example, African American men tend to over-indulge in cigarette, alcohol, and drug use, and to have limited participation in exercise and healthy eating habits. These behavior patterns adversely affect their health and are responsible for much of the premature morbidity and mortality in the African American male community.

Social policies must address behavioral risk factors such as cigarette smoking, alcohol and drug abuse, sexual practices, and interpersonal violence, in order for the health status of African American men to improve. More effective policies need to be developed to support culturally sensitive smoking cessation programs directed at African American men. The increasing rates of cancer among African American men suggest the need to examine cigarette use within this population. Cigarette smoking and alcohol abuse are, in fact, the leading cause of lung and esophagus cancer among African American men. While African American male children smoke at a lower rate than white male children, the statistics reveal that African American men are more apt to start smoking in their young adult years. According to the 1981 National Health Interview Survey, African American men between 18 and 24 years of age (24.9%) were less likely to smoke cigarettes than were their white counterparts (29.2%).[39] This pattern, however, is reversed for African American men throughout the remainder of the life cycle. Children of smokers are more prone than are children of non-smokers, to have respiratory illnesses and asthma, and infants of parents who smoke are more likely to die of sudden infant death syndrome than are infants whose parents do not smoke.[40] Substance abuse has also had an adverse impact on African American men and their families.[41]

Policy makers must also be more vigilant in regulating the alcohol and cigarette industries which are bombarding the African American community with advertising. Such advertising has increased in the African American community in recent years.[42] Social policies should be implemented to reduce excessive advertising of alcohol and cigarette products in the African American community. Further, drug policies in the United States should give greater priority to primary prevention. Limited funds are being allocated to alert African Americans to the adverse health risks of smoking and drinking.[43] Commenting on drug policies, Mason and his colleagues stated:

> Public substance abuse policies reflect an incoherent compromise between medical and criminal definitions and approaches to intervention. . . . Thus contemporary prevention, treatment and rehabilitation strategies fail to account for the myriad socioeconomic correlates of abuse and tend to atomize the problem by reducing it to the lowest common denominator—the drug-abusing persons.[44]

Based on these careful assessment of drug polices, they concluded:

> Primary prevention approaches to drug abuse hold the greatest promise for remediation of this social problem because of the inclusion of macroenvironmental factors in tandem with individual risk factors to form a comprehensive approach to policy formation.[45]

Overall, African American men suffer from higher rates of sexually transmitted diseases (STDs) than do white men.[46] More specifically, African American male homosexuals, bisexuals, and intravenous drug users have markedly higher rates of AIDS than do their white counterparts.[47] In addition, a recent study of African American adolescent crack users in San Francisco found that 41 percent reported having a history of sexually transmitted disease.[48] Recent data indicate that existing prevention programs have been grossly inadequate in alerting all sectors of the African American male community to the dangers posed by STDs, particularly AIDS. The National Commission on AIDS recently concluded that prevention programs have been designed and implemented without adequately considering the cultural and sexual habits of African American men.[49] It is, therefore, necessary to design innovative, culturally sensitive primary prevention strategies to help empower African American men and stop the spread of these diseases. In addition, social policies must begin to target media that promote unhealthy lifestyle practices, such as sexual irresponsibility.

The family can play an important role in promoting healthy life styles.[50] In 1985, the *American Health* magazine commissioned Gallup to conduct a survey to assess the way that families helped each other to be healthy.[51] The researchers examined factors that helped family members change their health behavior in a number of areas including: (1) quiting smoking; (2) exercising more; (3) cutting down on alcohol consumption; (4) controlling job stress; (5) losing weight; and (6) eating better. The primary question posed by the survey was whether the doctor or the family (including spouse or boyfriend or girlfriend) helped the respondent to change in any of the six behaviors above. In all areas, the respondents said the family played a more significant role than the doctor in health promotion. In fact, the family was reported to be twice as likely as the doctor to help reduce alcohol consumption. In addition, wives appeared to be more helpful than husbands in reducing alcohol consumption by their mates. Such research findings point to the need for programs that will encourage families to work together to reduce the incidence of substance abuse and addiction and to promote healthy life styles in general. Research in the realm of family health promotion, especially from the perspective of the family life of African American men, should be funded as part of social policy mandate.

NOTES

The Author would like to thank Mr. Christopher B. Booker and Ms. Roslyn G. Holmes for their technical assistance.

1. Na'im Akbar, *Visions for Black Men* (Nashville, TN: Winston-Derek Publishers, Inc., 1991); Lawrence E. Gary (ed.) *Black Men* (Beverly Hills, CA: Sage Publications, 1981) Jewelle Taylor Gibbs (ed.), *Young, Black and Male in American: An Endangered Species* (Dover, MA: Auburn House Publishing Company, 1988); Robert Staples, *Black Masculinity: The Black Male's Role in American Society* (San Francisco, CA: The Black Scholar Press, 1982); and Doris Y. Wilkinson and Ronald L. Taylor, *The Black Male in America* (Chicago, IL: Nelson-Hall, 1977).

2. Gibbs, *Young, Black and Male*.

3. Gibbs, *Young, Black and Male*; Haki R. Madhubuti, *Black Men: Obsolete, Single, Dangerous?* (Chicago, IL: Third Word Press, 1990); and Benjamin P. Bowser, ed., *Black Male Adolescents: Parenting and Education in Community Context* (Lanham, MD: University Press of America, 1991).

4. U.S. Bureau of the Census, *Statistical Abstract of the United States: 1992* (112th edition.) (Washington, DC: U.S. Government Printing Office, 1992).

5. Ibid., 76.

6. National Center for Health Statistics, *Health, United States, 1991* (Hyattsville, MD: Public Health Service, 1991), 140.

7. U.S. Bureau of the Census, *Statistical Abstract of United States: 1992*, 78.

8. U.S. Bureau of the Census, *Statistical Abstract of the United States: 1991* (Washington, DC: U.S. Government Printing Office, 1991), 75.

9. H. Carter and P. Glick, *Marriage and Divorce: A Social and Economic Study* (Cambridge, MA: Harvard University Press, 1976); David Mechanic, *Medical Sociology*, Second edition (New York: The Free Press, 1978), 162.

10. Michael Geerken and Walter R. Gove, "Race, Sex and Marital Status: Their Effect on Mortality," *Social Problems* 21 (1974): 567–580.

11. U.S. Bureau of the Census, *Statistical Abstract of the United States: 1992*, 44.

12. National Center for Health Statistics, *Health, United States, 1991*, 156.

13. Ibid.

14. Ibid.

15. Ibid.

16. Ibid.

17. Ibid.

18. Ibid.

19. Mechanic, *Medical Sociology*.

20. Ibid., 181.

21. Peter Ries, *Health of Black and White Americans, 1985–1987* (Hyattsville, MD: National Center for Health Statistics, 1990), 7.

22. Ibid., 45–46.

23. U.S. Department of Health and Human Services, *Health Status of Minorities and Low Income Groups*, 3rd edition (Washington, DC: U.S. Government Printing Office, 1991), 140–141.

24. National Center for Health Statistics, *Health, United States*; 1991, 210-212.

25. Ibid., 213.

26. Ibid., 214.

27. Ibid., 198.

28. Ibid., 156.

29. Ibid., 199.

30. Lawrence E. Gary and Dionne J. Jones, "Mental Health: A Conceptual Overview," in *Mental Health: A Challenge to the Black Community*, (ed.) Lawrence E. Gary (Philadelphia, PA: Dorrence and Company, 1978), 1-25; Sandra E. Taylor, "The Mental Health Status of Black Americans: An Overview," in *Health Issues in the Black Community*, (eds.) Ronald L. Braithwaite and Sandra L. Taylor (San Francisco, CA: Jossey-Bass Publishers, 1992), 20-34; and Walter L. Gove, (ed.) *Deviance and Mental Illness* (Beverly Hills, CA: Sage Publications, 1982).

31. Center for Mental Health Services and National Institute of Mental Health, *Mental Health, United States, 1992*, R.W. Manderschiel and M.A. Sonnenchein, (eds.) DDHHS Pub. No. (SMA) 92-1942 (Washington, DC: U.S. Government Printing Office, 1992), 284.

32. Ibid., 290.

33. Peter Ries, *Health of Black and White Americans, 1985–1987*, 45.

34. Ibid., 49.

35. National Center for Health Statistics, *Health, United States, 1991*, 219-220, 223.

36. U.S. Department of Health and Human Services, *Health Status of Minorities and Low-Income Groups*, 268.

37. Ibid., 268.

38. Peter Ries, *Health of Black and White Americans, 1985–1987*, 54, 55.

39. National Center for Health Statistics, *Health, United States, 1990* (Hyattsville, MD: Public Health Service, 1991), 124.

40. U.S. Department of Health and Human Services, *Reducing the Health Consequences of Smoking: 25 years of Progress, A Report of the Surgeon General* (Rockville, MD: Public Health Service, 1989).

41. Thomas D. Watts and Roosevelt Wright, eds., *Black Alcoholism: Toward a Comprehensive Understanding* (Springfield, IL: Charles C. Thomas, 1983; Bertha Mosely, Bobbie J. Atkins, and Michael Klein, "Alcoholism and Blacks," *Journal of Alcohol and Drug Education* 33 (1988): 51-58; and Oakley Ray and Charles Ksir, *Drugs, Society and Human Behavior*, Fourth edition (St. Louis, MO: Times Mirror/Mosby, 1987).

42. Reed V. Tuckson, "Race, Sex, Economics, and Tobacco Advertising," *Journal of the National Medical Association* 81 (November, 1989), 119-1224; and Watts and Wrights, *Black Alcoholism*.

43. Tuckson, "Race, Sex, Economics, and Tobacco Advertising."

44. Derek T. Mason, Mark W. Lusk and Michael Gintzler, "Beyond Ideology in Drug Policy: The Primary Prevention Model," *The Journal of Drug Issues* 22 (1992), 959-976.

45. Ibid., 959.

46. Dana Priest, "U.S. is Urged to View AIDS as a Racial Issue," *The Washington Post*, Tuesday, 12, January, 1993, sec. A.; C.R. Hayman and J.C. Probst, "Health Status of Disadvantaged Adolescents Entering the Job Corps Program, *Public Health Reports* 98 (1983): 369-376.

47. U.S. Department of Health and Human Services (1991). *Health Status of Minorities and Low-Income Groups*.

48. R.E. Fullilove, M.T. Fullilove, B.P. Bowser, and S.A. Gross, "Risk of Sexually Transmitted Diseases Among Black Adolescent Crack Users in Oakland and San Francisco, California," *JAMA: Journal of the American Medical Association* 263 (1990): 851.

49. Priest, "U.S. is Urged to View AIDS as a Racial Issue."

50. Perri J. Bomar, "Perspectives on family Health Promotion," *Family and Community Health* 12 (1990), 1-11.

51. Joel Gurin, "From "Me" to "We" The U.S. Generation," *American Health* 4 (1985), 40-41.

"Coolin": The Psychosocial Communication of African and Latino Men

Victor De La Cancela

It has been suggested that African American males emphasize "being cool" in behavior and attitude due to their lack of socioeconomic or political power. Given the historical and cultural connection between African Americans and United States Latino groups (e.g., Puerto Ricans), a brief theoretical exploration of the relationship between "machismo" and "cool pose" is conducted. It is suggested that both "masculine postures" can be used to design empowering psychological interventions in clinical, community and policy areas. Such masculine postures are examined as socioeconomic and historically related psychosocial survival mechanisms with both adaptive and maladaptive features. The positive features could be used to devise "inclusive curriculums of diversity" which might make schools, AIDS/HIV prevention and substance abuse treatment more relevant to males of color. Maladaptive features could similarly be identified to channel male youth into more constructive and empowering behavior.

Piri Thomas wrote that as a Black Puerto Rican youth growing up in the streets of New York, he mastered the art of masking and maintaining "la cara de palo" (the wooden face).[1] Thus, he appeared to be in control of his environment by presenting a blank screen to the external world. Majors, an African American psychologist, developed the thesis that African American males place great emphasis on "cool pose" as a behavior and attitude as a consequence of their being denied education, income or social, economic, and political power in the United States.[2] "Cool pose" is defined as a ritualized masculinity entailing scripts, posturing, impression management and other carefully constructed performances that present the male as proud, strong and in control.[3] "Cool pose" makes African American males visible and empowers them, yet it can also hide doubt, insecurity, rage and vulnerability, leaving males aloof from others and alienated from their deeper emotions.

Given that an analysis of "cool pose" provides enhanced understanding of the African American male experience, one wonders whether it can be applied to Latino men of African descent such as Puerto Rican males. Might study of "cool pose" and "machismo" be heuristic in fashioning models that explain survival strategies among men of color from different socioeconomic strata and which suggest empowering practical interventions?[4]

This article attempts to answer that question given the author's clinical observation and experiences with Latino men—men who are considered neither "Black" nor "white," and

33

who, along with other ethnics of color, struggle in "the promised land."[5] This work posits that the sociohistorical realities and economic experiences of peoples of African descent in the United States can explain current similarities and differences in African American and Puerto Rican use of "masculine protest" behaviors. While this article provides information primarily about Puerto Rican males, it may have important implications for other Latino men whose cultures have been significantly influenced by African peoples in parts of Latin America, i.e., Cuba, the Dominican Republic and other Caribbean regions.

FROM AFRICA TO THE "HOODS"

Reportedly, a form of "coolness" known as *ashe* existed in the practices of West African tribes such as the Yorubas of Western Nigeria circa 900 B.C.[6] The Yorubas, Bantus and Congos were among the tribes abducted and taken to Puerto Rico by the enslaving Spaniard colonizers after their extermination of the indigenous Taino inhabitants of *Borinquen* (the Taino name for Puerto Rico). Similar to the Aztecs in Mexico, the Tainos in Puerto Rico challenged the Spanish with acts of rebellion and suicide prior to their decimation. Similar "new world" struggles would occur in the United States and Caribbean years later as evidenced by African "slave" rebellions and uprisings.

The Puerto Rican emphasis on "salsa"[7] and the African American concept of "soul" are evidence of a contemporaneous struggle against the United States cultural mainstreaming or melting pot assimilation. Both represent cultural lifestyles and non-verbal communication that provide ethnic, racial, and psychosocial identity in the inner city "hoods" and *barrios*. *Danza, bomba* and *plena*, which are Latino African based dances, merge into new combinations with "house" and other dance styles. In African American and Latin Jazz, blues, gospel music and spirituals, we find popular/folkloric anthems for human rights, education, inspiration and skill acquisition toward group survival.[8]

On the East Coast, Machito, Ray Barreto, Eddie and Charlie Palmeri, Tito Puente, Mongo and Monguito Santamaria, and *mambo, cha-cha-cha, quaguanco, guajira*, and *meringue* have been part of the New York musical experience of Afro-Cubans, Puerto Ricans and African Americans for over five decades.[9] On the West Coast, Willie Bobo has won over R&B stalwarts with his *caliente* (hot) rhythms. This link of dancing and listening to the same music is an indicator of a shared legacy of the survival, presentation, and perseverance by peoples of African descent in the face of adversity. It is also significantly different from the tendency in the United States of African Americans and Caucasians to dance differently and to different music.[10]

Nowhere are these connections more obvious than in the primary development of rap music, breakdancing and graffiti art by African American and Latino/Puerto Rican male youth. Indeed, rap appears to have become the artistic expression of disenfranchised males of color, whether it is reggae rap or Spanish language rap in Puerto Rico or the Dominican Republic, or "spanglish" and bilingual rap among Chicanos and Panamanians. In each case, young males transcend poverty and lack of formal education, make new music with turntables, create songs, display verbal dexterity and "legitimately get paid."[11] Thus rapping provides the means to an income for African Americans and Latino youth today, as did early Latin rhythms and apartment parties for Puerto Rican New Yorkers in the 1930s.[12]

During the 1980s, dancing, especially breakdancing provided numerous adolescents of color opportunities for "hustling some change" on city street corners. Not only were onlookers amazed at the creativity of such performances, but choreographers, movie producers and advertisers also took note and recruited breakdancers and graffiti artists into their settings.[13] In fact, both art forms have been credited with saving many youth from "the streets." Breakdancing in particular is viewed as preventing inner city violence when it becomes a form of positive dance competition between males.[14]

COOL MACHOS AND DIALECTICS

"Cool pose" and other cultural expressions of males of African descent are not unilaterally positive. In fact, many observers are much more concerned with the negatives associated with the behaviors of male youth of color. The negatives are revealed through content analysis of rap lyrics, graffiti and dance styles. They are manifested by the "salsa" and "rap" entrepreneurs who pander "getting high," "partying," and sexually hedonistic attitudes.[15] Brand name consumerism among males of color is especially troubling to society as basketball shoes, designer label clothes, and the latest team jackets or leather coats become associated with threats, violence, and death.[16] Many social commentators argue, therefore, that "coolin" is replete with sexism, homophobia, criminality and racism.

It cannot be denied that "deviance" may be associated with "cool pose" and "machismo." However, these behaviors also reveal the importance of pride, dignity, respect and shame in African American and Latino Puerto Rican culture generally, and the man of color's subculture of survival specifically. An example of this dialectic is the current "gangster rap" genre and bragging that rappers routinely engage in, which is both contributory to adolescent conflict and reminiscent of games of "woofing," "playing the dozens," "sounding," "signifying" or "relajao" among African Americans and Puerto Ricans. These are games that teach males to maintain control and "keep cool" under the adverse conditions that they are likely to encounter as men of color in a racist society.

Dialectically attending to the rules, culture and symbols of gangs also reveals the importance of masculine rites of passage, solidarity, loyalty, conformity and identity attained through hand signals, language, clothing and being part of a "posse," "crew," or "family/familia." Related analysis of Rastafarian reggae and Nuyorican Poetry indicates that a "symbolic resignifying" exists in ethnocultural activities that share elements of marginal living and the invention of new survival strategies.[17] A dialectical and developmental theory of "coolin" would argue that with modifications made where necessary to avoid reinforcement of sexist, racist, criminal, homophobic or other anti-social ideology, the form, if not the substance, of these popular masculine expressions can be used to motivate youth towards progressive goals.

Illustrative of this is the Latin Empire, a "Puerto Rap" group avowedly singing to inform others about their culture, representing all Latinos and bringing different groups together.[18] African American rappers such as Chubb Rock and BDP who rhyme about racial self-help, stopping gang wars, distressing economic conditions, and the scourge of drug dealers can also be motivating. Even with their "macho" posturing, slang, "homeboy" dress styles, and "being down with hip-hop," these artists manifest "respeto" towards other rappers and their wider communities. These are youth who are not just bragging about themselves or "wearing gold," rather they are giving serious or positive tips on AIDS or violence. Other positive role models are African American and Latino "frat brothers" who style, vogue and wear status clothing, yet respect what others wear without abusing them for being different.[19] Both groups have one thing in common: the protagonists engage in the positive praxis of respect.

The themes of *respeto* (respect), *dignidad* (dignity), and pride among Puerto Rican males are central to understanding *machismo,* and may be helpful in conceptualizing "cool pose," "coolin" or "chillin." *Dignidad* basically requires the avoidance of loss of dignity before observers, while *respeto* signifies respect for authority, tradition and *familia.*[20] Another cultural value important in understanding Puerto Rican male behavior is *confianza*, a sense of confidence and trust that is essential to the establishment of positive interpersonal relationships. These values appear to originate from the Arabic impact on Spanish culture, specifically that heritage related to over 700 years of Arab presence in Spain, i.e., the Moors. Such values lead some Puerto Rican males to vigilantly defend against real or imagined insults to their sense of self worth and to avoid intimacy and kidding or joking around (*relajo*) until *confianza* has been established.

Among Puerto Rican youth on the mainland, this male ethos sometimes manifests itself in the value attached to being a "down brother," a "homey with heart" or "chill." Psychologists often view these youth as not self disclosing, avoiding social service/counseling programs, acting out, and covering up their feelings of insecurity because of and through these postures. Majors claims that similar "cool poses" among African American males have not been seriously considered as psychological defense or coping mechanisms utilized to counter stress and anxiety.[21] For example, "cool pose" may be used in therapy by African American males to keep mental health counselors and therapists, who are viewed as societal extensions of "the man," off-guard. The dynamic use of unique "cool" postures and behaviors can also offset a socially imposed "invisibility."[22] Folklorically, being "bad niggas," "cool dudes or cats" and acting with style and courage wins respect and status in the community.[23]

BEYOND MASCULINE CULTURE

Viewing "cool pose" as having both positive and negative attributes is necessary in order to overcome the more commonly held perception of it as a dysfunctional *cultural* version of "compulsively masculine" self-presentation. Even Majors and Billson place greatest emphasis on the way toughness and other masculine norms contribute to social problems and violence.[24] They, therefore, have not completely examined the economic, political and historical roots of social behaviors, problems and solutions among African American males.

Overstating of "cool pose" as causal in engendering sexual promiscuity, AIDS risk, military related mortality and morbidity, and illiteracy, among other social ills ignores the fact that these behaviors, similar to *machismo*, respond to specific socioeconomic and political realities. An adialectical focus on the negative gives the impression that these are solely the consequences of "personal choice" on the part of African American males and other men of color.[25] Rather, the positive and negative valencies of masculine roles among men of color can be understood in terms of their structural reality.

It is not only adherence to codes of toughness that serves as a barrier to visiting physicians or following prescribed regimes; there is also the real lack of access to and unavailability of health care in communities of color and lower socioeconomic status. Similarly, it is inappropriate to attribute the large number of African American, Puerto Rican, Chicano and Native American men in the military to an adherence to "macho" norms. Rather, the excess numbers and deaths of men of color in the armed forces are significantly related to limited economic and educational opportunities outside of the service, which attract "recruits" to a "volunteer" army. It is also true that poor people and people of color are targeted by armed forces recruiters. Moreover, class considerations and racism have also historically contributed to the draft and enlisted frontline status of "colored" men. Relating AIDS to sexual promiscuity among African American males without paying concomitant attention to intravenous drug use among these men is misleading. It is similarly misleading to relate "cool pose" to high teenage pregnancy rates and divorce rates without acknowledging that access to contraceptives, abortions, and sexual education and marital success among African Americans and European Americans differs in large part due to socioeconomic factors. In sum, it is inaccurate to engage in comparisons of Latino, African American and Caucasian male rates of domestic violence, homicide, gang activity, school suspension, detention or drop-out, and unemployment or incarceration, as if these groups are homogenous entities rather than the socioeconomically stratified groups that they are.

A more balanced picture of "cool pose" among African American and Latino males raises the class aspects of their existence and examines its potential for working class organization, education and the empowerment of youth. Among men of color, male behaviors have evolved into forms that can have a socially progressive intent even as a regressive sexism operates. Illustrative are the Black Power, Chicano and Puerto Rican movements of the mid-60s to the mid-70s. These have had a lasting impact on the political consciousness of some men of color, as manifested in contemporary African American and Latino leaders calling for similar affirmations of cultural and racial pride among youth. Additionally, public recognition of these activists is now occurring by mainstream organizations who see their own cultural-advocacy mission supported by these movements, e.g., ASPIRA and the Young Lords.[26]

TOWARD LATINO AND AFRICAN WARRIORHOOD

The Black Panther Party was "masculinist" in its outward militant, radical guerrilla appearance. Yet "machos" were credited with human service organizing throughout the country—in Chicago, Boston, Berkeley, and Watts. Their accomplishments such as free breakfast programs, political education/Black pride advocacy, promoting "Afro" self-respect, successful supermarket boycotts, and medical outreach made the Black Panthers positive forces in their neighborhoods.[27] Rather than viewing street corner dealers and gang members as the enemy, the Panthers saw these individuals as potentially rehabilitated and integrated into the struggle as liberation fighters.

On the west coast, *La Causa Chicana* looked to the *vatos* (gang members), *cholos* and *pachucos* and their unique language, dress style, lore and behaviors to integrate them into the movement.[28] New street organizations emerged with self-defense and community service orientations, such as the Brown Berets and *La Junta*. These primarily male youth groups emphasized cultural pride, study of *La Raza's* heritage, and identification with the renegades, rebels and revolutionaries of the Americas. They demanded bi-lingual education, community control of the police, and the right to bear arms. Their goal was to observe and protect *Raza* by all means necessary.

Movement youth intervened in *barrio* gang wars and negotiated peace, educating the *carnales* (brothers) and lowriders to whom the real enemy was. In fact, they were among the first to address Latino on Latino "homicide." As educators, they raised political consciousness and taught Spanish and English language skill development classes. As community organizers, they struggled against drug addiction, for educational reform, and for creative arts expression through poetry, theater, music, painting, and film. For example, *Los Comancheros del Norte*, from the mountain villages of New Mexico, declared "If you really were some kind of man, you would be fighting for your people. . . . We don't need machos." Political activists' platforms demanded a decent standard of living and an end to the preferential hiring of out-of-the community labor. Cesar Chavez appealed to Chicano manliness and brought God into the movement by asking for divine intervention in creating true, strong, and courageous men. Students, farmers and youth capable of self-sacrificing for others in non-violent struggle toward justice were to be the fruit of this heavenly harvest.[29]

In New York and Chicago, Puerto Rican male youth organized around the housing, health and social service needs of their communities. *Boricua* youth provided tuberculosis and lead poisoning detection programs, supported the struggles of welfare mothers, organized hospital workers, and operated day care centers. They condemned the impoverishment of Puerto Rican children, the psychological colonization of *la gente* (the people), and demonstrated and took over non-responsive institutions, e.g., churches, colleges, liberating them for *el pueblo*.[30]

The Young Lords published full-sized newspapers and produced a weekly FM radio program. Through improvements in sanitation collection, getting addicts to "kick their habits" and serve the people, and encouraging economic self-sufficiency, the Young Lords earned "respeto" from the community. Combatting racism and police brutality and struggling for prisoner rights, the Young Lords went from origins in street gangs to a definition of warriorhood, Rican power and class consciousness that evolved into a political party on the one hand, and a public service organization and developer of a Puerto Rican student movement, on the other.[31] At their height, the Lords had chapters in *el barrio*, Newark, the Bronx, the Lower East Side, Philadelphia, Bridgeport and Ponce, Puerto Rico.

The Lords and the Panthers have been justifiably criticized for their male chauvinism, yet their definition of *machismo* was dialectical as it called upon sisters in the struggle to be "down" and take a militant stand. In fact, one of the main areas the Young Lords targeted for change was male chauvinism and *machismo* among brothers in the movement. They also constructively criticized the passivity some women showed by allowing men to come out of their "superior attitudes bag." Such self-conscious activity led to an African American woman, Denise Oliver, being appointed to the Central Committee of the party and Minister of Finance.[32] Thus a new *machismo*, defined as the struggle of men and women everywhere for their independence, emerged.[33] Its composite identity was both progressive and reactionary, ranging from its crudest expression in the street gangs of the late 50s and early 60s, to a more movement friendly definition of pride and self-respect.[34]

Chicanos taking on *macho* characteristics, defined as vocal and aggressive community organizing, was also viewed as an important development in the civil rights struggle.[35]

More recently, a study of Mexican/Latino fathers reported that an androgynous view of *machismo* exists in which *macho* people are seen as being assertive, courageous and standing up for their rights.[36] Hence, in the midst of the "cool" posturing of African American and Latino male youth organizations of the 60s and 70s there emerged a critical, liberating and empowering view of *machismo* that contributed in part to women of color further developing as freedom fighters and leaders within those movements.

To examine "cool pose" or *machismo* as a dialectic is to view these behaviors as more than symbolic coping mechanisms. Historical analysis suggests they have contributed to organizing for civil rights, social justice, and instilling pride in people of color. They also have influenced criminal behavior, violence and some of the other ills Majors has identified. Ultimately, the issue is not whether "cool" posing in and of itself is cause or effect, but rather, what it does contribute to understanding the reality of men of color, and whether it can be helpful in improving their situation.

Commenting on African American youth's drug dealing and violence, some have spoken to the entrepreneurial aspects and economic imperatives of doing what you can to survive. As one author states: "these young men are not evil, they are making intelligent choices based on the options that are available to them: Burger King or the Posse."[37] DeLeon suggests focusing on the positive aspects of the African American male "hip-hop movement" with its innovation, artistic gains, political vision and Afro-centric identity, as well as its negatives, including sexism, materialism, and disrespect to fashion new youth leaders.[38]

EMPOWERING WITH COOL

Sociopolitical perspectives suggest that to "be cool" or "just chillin" is an attitudinal and behavioral script produced by some men of color (and variably reinforced by some women of color), that will be changed by men of color (and by women's demands on them), as their social circumstances dictate and as they challenge the economic and political conditions which keep their communities oppressed. Important in helping men of color understand the conflicted nature of their "cool pose," "coolin," or *machismo* is acknowledging the conflicted nature of the social realities they face within their lives.[39]

Connections to social reality and history help us to critically examine the portrayal of "cool pose" as an automatic function for many African American males.[40] It is important for those who work with men of color to make the psychosocial connection to survival, so that the negative self-limiting aspects of "coolin" and "chillin" can be clarified and understood in terms of their original function. It is inappropriate for psychologists to criticize or label racial, ethnic, cultural or class related male behaviors as pathological when they have neither enhanced understanding of how these behaviors emerged nor competently explored how to channel males into socioculturally viable alternatives.

Rather, mental health counselors can aid African and Latino males to historically and socioculturally reconstruct their masculine behavior by exploring the positive in their past individual and reference group histories. Teachers of color can emulate *griots* by sharing oral histories, their own learning and acquired survival skills with male youth of color. Elders, clergy and lay religious leaders, musicians, artists and activists have a responsibility, and the gifts and talents to help men of color to remember, unite, cleanse, purge, honor, and respect themselves and women.[41]

Progressive male writers and filmmakers, newspaper reporters and media broadcasters, whatever their racial background, must learn the lessons taught by feminism; namely, the importance of presenting new positive images and portrayals of people if we are to provide men and women of color an antidote for the poisoning self-hatred which they have been fed by a racist, sexist, and classist power elite. In fact, all of us, lawyers, corrections officers, human service workers, government funders, employers, legislators and policymakers, have important roles to play in the enrichment, enlightenment, mentoring, "womentoring" and empowerment of youth of color.

RECOMMENDATIONS TO ENRICH MEN OF COLOR

The following eight recommendations are made for increasing responsiveness in clinical, community and policy areas to Latino and African American men's realities. The recommendations are developed in response to Rose's (1991) call for the development of a proactive agenda for males of color that moves towards "enriching" them in the present and shaping a new reality for tomorrow.[42] In the spirit of this call, the following suggested responses are made to hasten the enrichment of males of color, especially that of our youth.

1.   Gay men of color can assume a more visible role in educating youth to how homophobia limits world views and the healthy development of their peers. Historical exploration of homosexuality in indigenous and old world cultures can challenge the view of homosexuality as a Caucasian manufactured deviation or genocidal plot that exists among some persons of color. Acknowledgment of the role played by Latino "drag queens" in the birth of the gay rights movement, i.e., Stonewall riots, can lead to exploration of how their *machismo* was being asserted. Exploration and acknowledgment of the longstanding contributions of lesbians of color to liberation and civil rights struggles can also occur. Latino gay men sharing how they deal with the negative legacy of *macho* child rearing can help build a sense of solidarity or commonality between youth and gay men. Latino gays can educate others regarding the way that gender posturing often occurs within the gay world, i.e., "tops," "bottoms," "bangees," "locas," "queens," etc.

2.   African American and Latino women must be included in manhood training programs developed for males of color because their contribution to ethnic racial group survival, both in economic and social terms, is significant. Mentoring programs should recognize that though men of color need a space for themselves and time to be with other men, women have important relationship building skills to model. Women of color have protected, cared for and enriched men even as they are overburdened by a "double minority" status related to gender and race. Like gays of color, whose double minority identity involves the issue of race and sexual orientation, women have much to share regarding how to deal with internal and external conflict. The inclusion of women in men's awareness programs also provides safeguards against the perpetuation of sexist attitudes by even well intentioned men.[43]

3.   Sexual and family violence (battering, incest, child abuse, rape, womanizing, verbal abuse) by African American and Latino/Puerto Rican males can be clearly portrayed as "uncool," or "lame to the bone." The male culture of silence which implicitly sanctions its occurrence needs to be broken. Men of color can learn that hurting their women and children is hurting themselves.[44] These behaviors might be challenged by

appealing to the concepts of nobility, ethics, and other internal qualities that some Latino males ascribe to being *macho*.[45] Health workers and activists can call for a "cease fire" that challenges men of color to confront themselves and each other to stop this intimate violence.[46]

4.   African and Latino youth can be provided "brotherhood" workshops that explore the commonalities between the two groups, e.g., their economic realities, and their significant differences with racial, linguistic, and institutional discrimination as a method of encouraging more responsible views of and relationships to their communities.[47] Discussions might include familial similarities (e.g., extended kinships and *compadraz-go*—co-parent systems), developmental similarities (e.g., how quickly young men of color lose their childhood), conflict resolution skills (e.g., how can they deal with anger or the daily micro-insults or disenfranchisement they face as African American and Latino men;[48] and of course, cultural and sociopolitical connections (e.g., rap, African legacy, "cool pose"). More therapeutically oriented group workshops might introduce the concept of the child within or inner child to help boys forced into manhood by their environment to understand unexplained feelings of abandonment and unexpressed desires to be cared for.[49]

5.   All adults who care about males of color can ask questions that "get into their head" such as: What does "being cool" or "chillin" mean to you? Can you give me an example (or examples) of someone you think is a real *macho* or man?[50] What kinds of things do men who are "down" do? Are any of those things self-destructive? Can you think of ways of being assertive or standing up for your rights that do not cause you or others harm? Other appropriate questions include: how does it feel to be a man today? To be a father, or worker? Is manhood honored, respected, celebrated?[51] How can a man of color be a strong man? The intent of such inquiry is to engage men in dialogue, a verbal communication that is respectful, empowering and promotes values clarification. Dialogue recognizes that the humane qualities men of color need to emulate are possessed by both genders alike and are essential for building community life.[52]

6.   The generally affluent urban Caucasian men's movement can examine how its concepts of experiencing the wild man within, dancing the warrior's dance, and other mythopoetic/metaphoric weekend gatherings may be failing Latino and African American men.[53] Critical to this examination is how the movement could be "ripping off" the cultural myths, rituals and practices of indigenous peoples globally such as sweat lodges, dancing, drumming, and council fires, and dangerously fashioning them into some pop, ersatz masculinity. The movement has also ignored current social conditions such as the fact that the majority of homeless people are men and the perpetuation of police brutality and harassment against both men of color and gay men.[54] It may well be that the anger and "ungrieved loss of manhood" that some low social economic status males and men of color experience is better engaged by exploration of native and pre-European intervention histories.[55] Study of slavery, fostered dependencies, and the dynamics of colonialism, racism, sexism, and classism, can aid men of color to explore understanding of themselves beyond where they are to where they can be.[56] It is paramount that examination of the economics, class, political power, and color privileges of middle-class Caucasian males occur, if men of color are to participate in men's movement events.

Additionally, the Bly-influenced men's movement includes women blaming tendencies, "patriarchal dualism" and pre-feminist understanding of gender issues that lead to so-called "soft men" being shunned for being emasculated by feminists and/or their mothers.[57] Men of color do not need to be further exposed to Caucasian males' unique form of male-bashing, racism, heterosexism and misogyny which has historically claimed that African American women castrate or feminize their men.

7.   Further research and study of the African American and Latino males' social realities is sorely needed to better understand how the stereotypes and perceptions applied to them by "mainstream" groups limit access to full participation within society. As Majors has indicated, misreading of the "cool pose" of African American youth has led to school suspension, detention, push-outs, etc., for where African American men feel they are communicating pride, strength and character, Caucasians see hostility, disrespect, threats and intimidation.

Media stereotypes of Latinos generally do not portray them as "cool," rather they are "hot," fiery, impassioned, emotional, excited, dangerous, quick-tempered spitfires, *machista* lovers and "caliente" dancers.[58] Thus, the question arises: How much of the Latino's subscription to "cool pose" is dependent upon the Latino's country or origin of ancestry, the male's own experiences of oppression, racism and economic limitation, the indigenous influences in their Latino sub-culture and dialects, and their migration experiences and proximity to African American communities and European American acculturation pressures? A hint of this heterogeneity is the fact that there was a minimal response by dark skinned Puerto Ricans on the island to the Black Power movement in the United States, while Puerto Ricans of all hues were highly involved in New York.[59]

8.   Teachers, counselors, juvenile justice and legal personnel can become competent in recognizing the different masculine self-definitions of African American and Latino men. Direct services to men of color can be enhanced when their *macho*, "cool pose" and "coolin" behaviors are not automatically viewed as a threatening deficit that must be eradicated or remedied.[60]

NOTES

1. P. Thomas, *Down These Mean Streets* (New York: Alfred A. Knopf, 1987).

2. R. Majors, "Cool Pose: A Symbolic Mechanism For Coping and Role Enactment Among Black Males." Unpublished manuscript, 1989.

3. R.G. Majors and J.M. Billson, (eds.) *Cool Pose: The Dilemmas Of Black Manhood In America* (New York: Lexington Books, 1992).

4. V. De La Cancela "A Critical Analysis of Puerto Rican Machismo: Implications For Clinical Practice, *Psychotherapy, 23(2)* (1986): 291-296; De La Cancela "Labor Pains: Puerto Rican Males In Transition," *El Boletin: Centro de Estudios Puertorriquenos Bulletin* (Fall, 1988): 41-55.

5. C. Brown *Manchild In the Promised Land* (New York: Macmillan, 1965).

6. W. Bascom, *The Yoruba of Southwestern Nigeria* (New York: Rinehart and Winston, 1969).

7. V. De La Cancela, "Salsa And Control: An AmeRican Response To Latino Health Care Needs," *Journal of Multi-Cultural Community Health* 1(2), (1991): 23-29.

8. Ibid.

9. M. Salazar, "Latin Music: The Perseverance Of A Culture." In C.E. Rodriquez, V. Sanchez Korral, & J.O. Alers (eds.). *The Puerto Rican Struggle: Essays On Survival In The U.S.* (New York: Puerto Rican Migration Research Consortium, Inc., 1980), 74-81.

10. C.E. Rodriquez, "Puerto Ricans: Between Black And White. In Rodriquez et. al. (eds.) *The Puerto Rican Struggle*, 20-30.

11. J. Pareles, "On Rap, Symbolism And Fear." *The New York Times* (February 2, 1992).

12. Salazar, "Latin Music."

13. R. Majors, "Nonverbal Behaviors and Communication Styles Among African Americans." In R. Jones (ed). *Black Psychology*, (3rd Edition), (Berkeley, CA: Cobb & Henry, 1991), 269-294.

14. Ibid.

15. P. Guzman, "Puerto Rican Barrio Politics In the United States." In Rodriquez, et al (eds.) *The Puerto Rican Struggle*, pp. 121-128.

16. Majors, "Non Verbal Behaviors And Communication Styles."

17. A.G. Quintero-Rivera, "Culture-Oriented Social Movements: Ethnicity And Symbolic Action In Latin America And the Caribbean,"*Centro De Estudios Puertorriquenos Bulletin,*3 (2),(1991): 97-104.

18. J. Flores, "Latin Empire: Puerto Rap." *Centro De* Estudios Puertorriquenos Bulletin. 3(2), (1991): 77-85.

19. Majors, "Nonverbal Behaviors And Communication Styles."

20. E.W. Christensen, "Counseling Puerto Ricans: Some Cultural Considerations." *Personnel And Guidance Journal,*(January, 1975): 349-355.

21. R. Majors, "Cool Pose: A Symbolic Mechanism For Masculine Role Enactment Among Black Males." Paper presented at 67th Annual Meeting of the American Orthopsychiatric Association, Miami, April, 1990.

22. R. Ellison, *Invisible Man* (New York: Signet Books, 1947).

23. R. Milner, "The Trickster, The Bad Nigger, And The New Urban Ethnography: An Initial Report And Editorial Code," *Urban Life And Culture,* 1 (1972): 109-117.

24. Majors, "Cool Pose: A Symbolic Mechanism." Majors and Billson.

25. B. Erazo Vazquez, Personal Communication. Centro De Estudios, Puertorriquenos, Hunter College, City University of New York, March 1990.

26. J. Rice, *The ASPIRA Story: 1961-1991* (Washington, DC: ASPIRA Association, Inc., 1991).

27. A. Shepard, "Remember the Black Panthers and Their Cause," *Free My People: Newsletter of Free My People/Youth Leadership Movement*, (October 1989), 1-2.

28. L. Valdez and S. Steiner (eds.) *Aztlan: An Anthology of Mexican American Literature* (New York: Vintage Books, 1972).

29. C. Chavez, "God Help Us to be Men," in L. Valdez and S. Steiner (eds.) *Aztlan: An Anthology of Mexican American Literature*, p.386.

30. M. Abramson and Young Lords Party, *Palante—Young Lords Party* (New York: McGraw-Hill Book Company, 1971).

31. Rice, *The ASPIRA Story*.

32. Abramson and Young Lords Party, *Palante—Young Lords Party*.

33. S. Steiner, *The Islands: The Worlds of Puerto Ricans* (New York: Harper and Row, 1974).

34. A. Lopez, *The Puerto Rican Papers: Notes on the Re-emergence of a Nation* (New York: Bobbs-Merrill Co., 1973)

35. L. Aguilar, "Unequal Opportunity and the Chicana," *Civil Rights Digest* 5, 4 (1973): 30-33.

36. A. Mirande, "Que Gacho es Ser Macho: It's a Drag to be a Macho Man," *Atzlan: The Journal of Chicano Studies* 17, 2 (1986): 63-89.

37. A. DeLeon, "Not the Enemy," *Free My People: Newsletter of Free My People/Youth Leadership Movement* (October 1989), 6.

38. Ibid.

39. G. Strickland and L. Holzman, "Developing Poor and Minority Children as Leaders with the Barbara Taylor School Educational Model," *Journal of Negro Education* 55,3 (1989): 383-398.

40. R.G. Majors, "Cool Pose: A New Approach Toward a Systematic Understanding and Study of Black Male Behavior." Unpublished Doctoral Dissertation, University of Illinois, Urbana-Champaign, 1987.

41. V. De La Cancela, "The Endangered Black Male: Reversing the Trend for African American and Latino Males," *Journal of Multi-Cultural Community Health* 1, 1 (1991): 16-19.

42. B. Rose, "The Endangered Black Male: A Perspective for Enrichment," *Journal of Multi-Cultural Community Health 1, 1* (1991):13-15.

43. A.R. Powell, Personal Communication, 1992.

44. B.Y. Avery, "Breathing Life into Ourselves: The Evolution of the National Black Women's Health Project," In E.C. White (ed.), *The Black Women's Health Book: Speaking for Ourselves* (Washington: Seal Press, 1990).

45. Miranda, "Que Gacho es Ser Macho"; F.J. Guittierez, "Exploring the Macho Mystique: Counseling Latino Men. In D. Moore and F. Leafgreen (eds.), *Problem-solving Strategies and Interventions for Men in Conflict* (Alexandria, VA: American Association of Counseling and Development Press, 1990), pp. 131-159.

46. B. Shuchter, "Cease-Fire: A Call for Men to Stop Violence Against Women," *Boston Area Rape Crisis Center Newsletter*, May 1990, 4.

47. V. De La Cancela, "Keeping African American and Latino Males Alive: Policy and Program Initiatives in Health," *Journal of Multi-Cultural Community Health* 2, 1 (1992): 31-39.

48. I. Wilkerson, "Facing Grim Data on Young Males: Blacks Grope for Ways to End Blight," *New York Times*, July 17, 1990, A14.

49. Guittierez, "Exploring the Macho Mystique."

50. Mirande, "Que Gacho es Ser Macho."

51. F.E. Neller, "Tough Guys and Teddy Bears (A Glimpse at the Warrior Within)," *Recovery Press* 3,3 (1992): 11-12.

52. Powell, Personal Communication.

53. R. Cabezas, "Miserable Failure," *Wingspan: Journal of the Male Spirit* (April-June 1991): 2.

54. H. Schuchman and D. McGraw-Schuchman, The Re-making of Men," *Readings: A Journal of Reviews and Commentary in Mental Health* 7, 2 (1992): 14-19.

55. M. Laureano and E. Poliandro, "Understanding Cultural Values of Latino Male Alcoholics and Their Families: A Culture Sensitive Model," *Journal of Chemical Dependency Treatment Initiatives* 4, 1 (1991): 137–155.

56. N. Akbar, *Visions for Black Men* (Nashville, TN: Winston-Derek Publishers, Inc., 1991).

57. S. Doubiago, "Enemy of the Mother: A Feminist Response to the Men's Movement," *Ms.* (March/April 1992): 82–85; J. Johnston, "Why Iron John is No Gift to Women," *New York Times Book Review* (February 23, 1992), 1.

58. E. Fernandez, "Spitfires, Latin Lovers, Mambo Kings," *New York Times*, April 19, 1992, Section 2, 2.

59. Rodriguez, "Puerto Ricans: Between Black and White."

60. Majors and Billson, *Cool Pose: The Dilemmas.*

Stressful Life Events, Psychosocial Resources, and Depressive Symptoms Among Older African American Men[1]

Gayle D. Weaver and Lawrence E. Gary

Empirical studies focusing on the mental health of older African American men are sparse. This article examines the relationship of depressive symptoms to demographic factors, stressful life events, and psychosocial coping resources in a sample of 161 African American men 56 years of age and over. The multivariate analyses demonstrate a significant association between depressive symptomatology and household income, stressful life events, number of illnesses, mastery over the immediate environment, and self-rated health. Men who were least at risk for high depressive symptoms had incomes above $25,000, experienced few or no stressful life events and physical illnesses, and reported high mastery and health ratings. Implications of the findings are discussed relative to future research and mental health service needs.

After more than 25 years of research on the relationships among stressful life events, social and psychological resources, and physical and mental health, it is unfortunate that so little is known about how these relationships impact on African American males, particularly the elderly segment of the population. It is unfortunate because they are at high risk for many of the nation's leading health threats, including heart disease, cancer, hypertension, stroke, and homicide, all of which have been linked to stressful environments and inadequate support resources.[2]

The available literature on African American men indicates that they experience comparatively more negative life events such as unemployment and underemployment, economic insecurity, low educational attainment, police harassment, criminal victimization, and incarceration than do white males.[3] In addition, there is evidence suggesting that experiences of stress among African Americans start earlier in life and are greater in number, wider in range, endured for longer periods, and more frequent compared to their white counterparts.[4] Myers argues that the objective realities of race and class prejudices and discrimination create a high basal stress level among African Americans which may account for the increased risks for disease, instability, and death.[5]

The African American elderly male population has been referred to as an "invisible minority within a minority."[6] According to Kart, the emphasis on the double jeopardy and triple jeopardy hypotheses has resulted in a predominance of studies on this population as a whole or on African American women only.[7] As a consequence, the limited attention to older African American men perpetuates the assumption that this group is homogeneous. However, sociodemographic and health profiles provided by Kart and others clearly illustrate that differences exist among elderly African American males.[8] While recognizing these differences, it is also important to acknowledge this group's propensity for survival. Their disadvantaged status throughout history has generated the development of problem-solving skills that have enabled these men to survive the odds. Documentation of their unique difficulties and coping strategies will foster a better understanding of the determinants of health, and result in culturally appropriate services.

The present study explores differences in mental health among older African American men. It assumes that this population of men is heterogeneous and that demographic characteristics, stress, and coping resources all contribute to the intragroup variation in their mental health. More specifically, the objectives of this article are to examine: a) the relationship of depressive symptomatology to sociodemographic factors, stressful life events, and psychosocial coping resources; and b) the extent to which these factors predict depressive symptomatology. While the study focuses on a small number of older men, it will provide insight into the degree and importance of intragroup diversity in mental health and its correlates among older African American men. Moreover, it will be useful to mental health programs in identifying groups potentially "at risk" for mental health problems.

PREVIOUS RESEARCH

Despite the relative inattention to elderly African American men, prior research on African American men in general and the larger African American population provides a framework for examining differences in mental health. Studies conducted by Brown and Gary, Dressler and Badger, Tran et al., and Husaini et al. reveal important variations in mental health on the basis of gender, age, socio-economic status, stressful life events, and several other psychosocial factors.[9] For example, Dressler and Badger's comparison of epidemiologic data on depressive symptoms from three African American communities (southern-rural, midwestern and western-urban) indicate inter- and intra-community differences as a function of sociodemographic factors.[10] The key findings of this study revealed generally low prevalence rates of depressive symptoms for males across the three communities. However, the rates were much lower for men in rural Alabama than they were for men in Kansas City and Alameda County. Surprisingly, in the last two communities, the rates for males were slightly higher than those for females. An explanation for the variability across the communities in male rates is not offered, but it is possible that males in urban areas are apt to lead more stressful and unstable lives than their rural counterparts. As suggested by Dressler and Badger, regarding the effects of income on depression rates, there may be more supportive networks for males in the southern community than for those in those in the western and mid-western urban areas.

Intragroup variation linked to gender and mental health has also been investigated by Brown and Gary.[11] Their study focused on how depressive symptomatology and its relationship to social support differs in 451 urban African American men and women from the mid-Atlantic region. They found that the men reported significantly fewer depressive symptoms, more neighborhood ties, and lower religious involvement than did the women. Among the six social support factors examined, none significantly predicted depressive symptoms for males. For females, however, nearby relatives and satisfaction with social support were important predictors of depressive symptoms. Interestingly, this study illustrates differences in depressive symptoms as a function gender, while the lack of significant correlates of depressive symptoms for the men denotes a need for research of an ethnographic nature which will identify factors that are important to African American men's well-being.

In reviewing the literature, only one study was found that examined within-group differences in depressive symptoms among African American men.[12] Similar to the work of Dressler and Badger, Gary's research of 142 African American men showed that depressive symptoms vary as a function of sociodemographic factors and sociocultural factors. Men who were under age 30, had low family incomes (8,000), lived in large households, were unemployed, and experienced stress in their intimate relationships reported the highest levels of depressive symptoms. However, a multivariate analysis showed that conflict with mates and family income accounted for much of the variation in symptomatology. As in the studies mentioned previously, the social support variables (i.e., religious involvement, friend networks, and community participation), generally considered vital to the survival of African Americans, were found to be insignificant to their well-being. Although not statistically significant, several trends in Gary's findings indicated that the small number of men who moved often, had several arrests, and lived in extended households were at risk for high symptomatology.

Thus far, research has focused on the larger adult African American population. What, then, do we know about the mental health of the elderly segment? To date, only a few studies have explored intragroup differences among aged African Americans and even these have not focused on older men, despite their social conditions which qualify them as a vulnerable group.[13] Tran, Wright and Chatters' investigation of the relationships among health, stress, psychological resources, and subjective well-being in a sample of 581 older African Americans is one exception to this rule of omission.[14] Their study revealed that poor subjective well-being was associated with low levels of personal efficacy, perceived poor physical health, and stressful life events. Moreover, their findings indicated that income, education, gender, marital status, and age were not important determinants of subjective well-being. Due to the inconsistent findings regarding sex differences, the researchers chose not to examine these relationships separately for men and women.

Husaini and his associates' study of a sample of 600 southern, aged African Americans, however, represents one attempt to specify the influence of gender differences on the relationships among depressive symptoms, stress, coping resources, and physical health problems.[15] Their findings corroborated those of Brown and Gary. They found symptomatology among the males to be associated with a greater number of medical problems and poor ego (i.e., executive ability and tension control). For females, however, several factors were important: chronic medical problems, poor ego, low support, and low contact with relatives and friends. Consistent with other findings, life events were not significant correlates of depressive symptoms for their sample.[16]

The present study is, therefore, timely in that it provides evidence on the impact of stress and psychosocial resources on the mental health of older African American men.

METHODS

Sample

The data used in this investigation are from the Norfolk Area Health Study (NAHS).[17] The NAHS consists of a representative sample of 1,018 African American adult males and females living in Norfolk, Virginia 18 years of age and older. A multi-stage, cluster sampling design was employed to select potential respondents. Face-to-face interviews of approximately two hours in length were conducted by trained interviewers in the respondents' homes. This study used data from the 161 males aged 56 years and over to examine the issue of diversity in mental health among older African American men.

With respect to marital status, 62.3 percent of the men were married, 15.1 percent were divorced or separated, 13.2 percent were widowed, and 9.4 percent were never married. Although household incomes were varied, the largest percentage of men reported incomes less than $10,000 (32%); 26 percent had incomes between $10,000 and $14,999; 27 percent had incomes in the $15,000 to $24,999 range; and 15 percent reported incomes at or above $25,000. Over half of the respondents had attained 8 years or less of schooling (58%), while 17 percent had attained 9 to 11 years, 8 percent had completed high school, and 17 percent had some college background. Most of the respondents were not working (68%) at the time of the interview.

Measures

Depressive Symptoms. The Center for Epidemiologic Studies Depression Scale (CES-D) was used to measure depressive symptoms.[18] The CES-D consists of a 20-item self-report symptom scale that taps the level of depressive symptomatology during the preceding week. It is based on feelings or moods such as guilt, worthlessness, helplessness, loss of appetite and sleep disturbance. Total scores can range from 0 to 60, with scores at or above 16 representing high depressive symptomatology. The mean score for this sample was 10.80 (SD=8.07). The Cronbach alpha coefficient was .82, indicating good internal consistency.

Demographic Factors. The demographic factors included marital status, household income, education, and employment status. Household income was based on the total income of all persons residing in the home; education was measured by the highest number of years of schooling completed; and employment status was based on whether or not the respondent currently held a job.

Stressful life events. Three measures were used to assess stressful life events. The first, Recent Life Changes Questionnaire (RLCQ) measured stress from acute, *major life events.*[19] The RLCQ consists of 76 items which cover five areas: health, work, home and family, personal and social matters, and financial concerns. Respondents were asked if any of these events had happened to them during the past year. The total major life events score was based on a sum of events experienced. An average of 6.19 (SD=6.12) major life events were reported. The most commonly reported major stressful life events (i.e., reported by at least 25% of the men) included the death of close family and friends, increase in income, taking on moderate debt, change in eating habits, and change in personal habits.

Chronic or *daily stressful life events* were assessed using the modified version of the Hassles Scale.[20] This scale consists of 59 items in the areas of work, health, family, friends, the environment, chance occurrences, and practical considerations. Respondents were asked to indicate whether or not they had any of the daily hassles during the past month. A sum of the items checked constituted the daily hassles score. The mean number of hassles reported was 6.46 (SD=6.16). Commonly reported daily life events for these men included concerns about physical shape, money emergencies, necessities and extras, medical care, and overall health.

The last measure of stressful life events focused on the *physical conditions* experienced by respondents. Using a list of 20 illnesses and conditions, they were asked to indicate the type and number of major physical illnesses or conditions that limited their ability to be active during the past six months. Illnesses reported by respondents not on the list were also included. An average of 1.43 (SD=1.12) medical conditions were reported by the respondents. The most frequently reported conditions included arthritis, poor vision, and hypertension.

Psychosocial resources. Five psychosocial coping resources were examined: mastery, emotional support, self-rated health, community participation, and church involvement. Resources are believed to have health enhancing effects whether or not in times of change or stress.[21] *Mastery* or perceptions of control over the occurrence of events in one's life was assessed by Pearlin and Schooler's Mastery Scale.[22] This scale consists of seven statements representing feelings or attitudes that people have concerning control over the events that befall them, solving their problems, and directing their future. Respondents were asked to indicate on a 4-point scale the extent to which they agreed or disagreed with the statements. The score was from 0 to 21, with a high score indicating perceived mastery over their environment. The mean mastery score for this sample was 14.71 (SD=4.02), indicating that these men felt some degree of mastery. The Cronbach alpha coefficient was .71.

The Inventory of Socially Supportive Behaviors (ISSB) developed by Barrera, Sandler, and Ramsay was employed to measure *emotional support*.[23] The items comprising this inventory assessed the self-reported frequency of a variety of supportive behaviors (i.e., informational, tangible or instrumental, emotional, and integrational) provided by others. However, for the purposes of this study, only those items related to the receipt of emotional support from the family and friend networks were used. Based on Krause and Markides' maximum likelihood factor analysis of the ISSB in a multi-ethnic sample of older adults, the emotional support subscale was one of four scales that emerged.[24]

This subscale consists of 14 items which focused on having someone to: stay with you in stressful situations, do some activity with you, listen to you talk about private feelings, express interest in your welfare, and so on. Respondents were asked to indicate on a 5-point scale how often their closest network members did each of the 14 activities for or with them during the previous month: 0-not at all, 1-once or twice, 2-about once a week, 3-several times a week, or 4-about everyday. The score range was 0 to 64. The subscale's internal consistency was high, Cronbach alpha = .91. The mean score for this sample was 20.64 (SD=12.96), indicating a somewhat low level of emotional support from close network members.

Among the factors examined here, the literature indicates that physical health status would have the strongest relationship to mental health.[25] Research typically shows that poor physical health is associated with poor mental health.[26] The respondents' *self-rated health* was included as an indicator of perceived physical functioning. They were asked to rate their physical health on a 4-point scale as either 3-excellent, 2-good, 1-fair, or 0-poor. Clearly, this single-item measure does not capture the variability of multiple physical health indicators. But, there is a strong evidence documenting its high correlation with physicians' ratings and individuals' later health status.[27] The mean perceived health rating was 1.58 (SD=1.06), indicating that the men generally felt their health was fair.

Participation in community activities is viewed as a potential avenue of support and its importance for mental well-being has been documented.[28] Through community participation, various informal and formal resources can be utilized in coping with the daily activities of living. For example, individuals can rely upon their neighbors, fraternal and sororal organizations, and service groups for a variety of supports. The *community participation* variable consisted of the number and type of organizational memberships.[29] Respondents were asked to indicate if they belonged to nine organizations such as social clubs, fraternal groups, political groups, civic or service clubs. In addition to organizational membership, respondents were asked if they voted in the last (1984) presidential election. The community participation score simply represented the total number of memberships. The mean score was 2.09 (SD=1.69).

The last psychosocial resource examined was *church involvement*. Throughout history, the church has functioned in numerous ways in African American communities.[30] The African American church has been portrayed as a protector for slaves, an economic source, sponsor of education, and political organizer. This variable was measured by asking respondents to indicate how often they attend religious services, using a 5-point scale. The responses could range from rarely or never (0) to once a week or more (4). The men reported an average of 2.86 (SD=1.25). Thus, church attendance for this group was about two to three times a month or more.

DATA ANALYSIS

Oneway analysis of variance (ANOVA) was used to test intragroup differences in mental health and multiple regression analysis was performed to determine the direct influences of stressful life events and psychosocial resources on depressive symptoms, controlling for demographic variables. Age was included in the regression equation as a control variable because of the wide age range in the sample—from ages 56 to 91. It must be noted that number of illnesses and self-rated health indicators were only analyzed at the multivariate level. Furthermore, education and employment status were eliminated from the regression analysis due to their insignificant contribution to the explained variance in depressive symptoms. To reduce possible confounding between stressful life events and depressive symptoms measures, items relating to changes in sleeping and eating habits were removed from the RLCQ. The modified Hassles scale was developed in response to the controversy surrounding this issue.

RESULTS

Demographics and Depressive Symptoms

As can be seen from the data reported in Table 1, each of the demographic variables was significantly associated with depressive symptomatology. The highest levels of depressive symptoms were reported by men who were divorced/separated or were never married, had incomes below $10,000, had less than 12 years of schooling, and were working. Among these men, two categories of men appeared to be at risk of high symptomatology: those who were divorced or separated and those who had incomes between $6,000 and $9,999. Both groups had mean scores above the 16-point cut-off. The men least at risk included those who had household incomes at or above $25,000 and some college background. These men typically reported scores below seven points.

Stressful Life Events and Depressive Symptoms

Table 1 also shows significant associations between the stressful life events measures and depressive symptoms. As expected, men who reported high levels of major life events ($F(2,158)=8.74$, $p<.01$) and daily hassles ($F(2,137)=15.24$, $p<.01$), also reported a high level of depressive symptomatology. Depression scores, however, tended to be higher when daily hassles were experienced. Thus, men at risk of high symptomatology were those with a high level of hassles.

Psychosocial Resources and Depressive Symptoms

Of the four resources analyzed at the bivariate level, mastery ($F(2,152)=8.22$, $p<.001$), emotional support ($F(2,144)=4.45$, $p<.01$), and community involvement ($F(2,158)=3.39$, $p<.05$) were significantly associated with depressive symptoms. Based on the analyses, the lowest depression scores were reported by men who had high levels of emotional support and community involvement, and a moderate level of mastery. High depression scores were reported by men with low mastery, and moderate community involvement and emotional support, but none approached the 16-point cut-off. Although church involvement was not significantly related to depressive symptoms, there were slight differences in the scores of men who attended church on a regular basis and those who attended less often.

Predictors of Depressive Symptoms

Table 2 presents the results of the multiple regressions. In testing the direct effects of stressful life events, it was found that all three stress sources were significant predictors of symptomatology. The results indicated that low household incomes, increased major life events, increased daily hassles, and the presence of physical illnesses were significantly associated with increased depressive symptomatology. The stressful life events equation accounted for 29 percent of the explained variance ($F(6,154)=12.11$, $p<.001$).

TABLE 1
Depressive Symptoms by Independent Variables

Characteristics	N	M	SD
Marital Status ***			
Married	99	9.48	7.78
Divorced/separated	24	16.18	8.20
Widowed	21	9.68	5.01
Never married	15	13.67	9.49
Household income**			
≤$6,000	23	13.66	1.98
$6,000–9,999	16	16.44	2.36
$10,000–14,999	32	9.57	1.20
$15,000–24,999	33	9.47	1.35
≥$25,000	18	6.71	1.43
Education**			
8 years	92	11.82	8.64
9–11 years	27	12.47	8.33
12 years	13	7.52	5.33
some college	27	6.88	5.29
Employment Status*			
working	49	11.82	8.66
not working	106	8.70	5.88
Major Life Events***			
none	15	7.23	6.51
some (1–3)	79	8.97	7.37
high (4+)	67	13.75	8.32
Daily Hassles***			
none	30	5.98	5.40
some (1–3)	76	9.85	7.71
high (4+)	36	15.67	7.64
Mastery***			
low	63	13.70	9.66
medium	44	8.16	5.78
high	48	9.05	6.28
Emotional Support**			
low	64	10.82	8.40
medium	51	12.75	7.91
high	32	7.44	6.68
Community Involvement*			
none	19	10.55	5.87
some (1–2)	100	11.96	8.66
high (3+)	42	8.15	6.92
Church Involvement			
rarely or never	28	10.90	6.70
several times a year	33	13.16	8.76
weekly	98	9.05	6.28

* $p<.05$ ** $p<.01$ *** $p<.001$

TABLE 2
Depressive Symptoms Regressed on Stressful Life
Events and Psychosocial Resources[a,b]

Variables	R	R^2Change	Beta
A. Stressful Life Events			
Age	-.08	.01	-.06
Income	-.29***	.10	-.19**
Marital Status	-.23**	.01	-.11
Major life events	.29***	.08	.21**
Daily hassles	.39***	.08	.26***
# Illnesses	.34***	.04	.21**
Total R^2		.32	
Adjusted R^2		.29	
F(6,154)=12.11***			
B. Psychosocial Resources			
Age	-.08	.01	-.14
Income	-.29***	.10	-.11
Marital status	-.23**	.01	-.10
Mastery	-.36***	.07	-.21**
Self-rated health	-.35***	.04	-.23**
Church involvement	-.09	.00	.09
Emotional support	-.13*	.02	-.13
Community involvement	-.23**	.01	-.14
Total R^2		.26	
Adjusted R^2		.22	
F(1,152)=6.66**			

* p<.05   ** p<.01   *** p<.001
[a] A dummy code was used for marital status: married=1, not married=0.
[b] Standardized regression coefficients are reported.

While the explained variance is less for the psychosocial resources (R^2=.22), their contribution is statistically significant ($\underline{F}$(8,152)=6.66, p<.01). Within this equation, demographic factors are not significant and only two of the resources are important contributors to the variance in depressive symptoms. Mastery and self-rated health emerged as the significant predictors of depressive symptoms. Declines in symptomatology were significantly related to positive health ratings and perceived mastery. It is important to highlight that the wide age variance in this group did not appear to affect variation in depressive symptoms.

DISCUSSION

The aims of this study were to examine the extent of intragroup differences in the mental health of older African American men, as well as to specify the relationships among depressive symptoms, socio-demographic factors, stressful life events, and psychosocial resources. Support for Kart's assertion that older African American men are a heterogeneous group was obtained in this investigation. According to the bivariate analyses, all of the variables under study were significantly related to depressive symptomatology, except age and church attendance. In brief, it was found that fewer depressive symptoms were associated with being married or widowed, high household incomes, 12 years or more of schooling, not working, few or no major and daily life stressors, perceptions of moderate to high mastery, perceptions of good to excellent health, and high community involvement and emotional support. Considering the supportive role of the church in African American communities, it was surprising to find no significant relationship between church attendance and mental health. The trend, however, was in the expected direction; that is, fewer depressive symptoms were reported by men who attended church on a weekly basis.

At this level of analysis, the findings indicate that some older men are more at risk for symptomatology than are others. While further systematic research is needed to explore mental health differences among this specific subgroup, it is felt that these findings provide strong support for accepting the intragroup difference notion. Moreover, it is felt that such findings should be incorporated into policy which will lead us away from "standardized" services to more age-, gender- and culturally-appropriate mental health services.

When the multivariate analyses are considered, a different picture emerges of the variables that are important for symptomatology. Among the twelve variables analyzed, only six explained significant portions of the variance in depressive symptoms: household income, major life events, daily hassles, the presences of illnesses, mastery, and self-rated health. It appears, then, that the mental health of this sample was most affected by objective conditions as indicated by income and stressful life events, and psychological and health resources (i.e., perceived mastery and health status). Thus, service providers may need to target those older men who have few economic resources, are under high stress, and have inadequate psychosocial resources.

Overall, this study partially corroborates the findings of previous work on African Americans. Similar to the studies conducted by Tran et al. and Markides et al., the socio-demographic factors, on a whole, were not predictive of depressive symptoms.[31] One interpretation for this finding is that demographic factors, particularly socio-economics, decline in their importance with advancing age because of selective survival. According to this thesis, members of socio-economically disadvantaged groups are more likely to die early, thus making such measures less predictive of health outcomes,[32] particularly mental health outcomes.

Regarding the effects of stressful life events, studies conducted by Husaini et al. and Brown and Gary found major life events to be insignificant.[33] In this study, both major life events and daily hassles were predictive of depression. The effect of the presence of physical illnesses, however, was consistent with the work of Husaini et al. and Tran et al. In addition, our findings on coping resources were consistent with those of Husaini et al.

For example, emotional support from family and friends, community involvement, and church attendance were of little use to the men. But perceived mastery over the environment and perceived good physical health were found to decrease the risks for symptomatology. Husaini et al. reported that the absence of medical problems and high ego strength were associated with low depression. It appears that men are likely to rely more on their internal strengths than on their external supports in maintaining or improving their mental health.

NOTES

1. Parts of this paper were presented at the Conference on Health and Social Behavior of African American Males, Howard University, Washington, D.C. (October 1991).

2. Department of Health and Human Services, *Health Status of Minorities and Low-Income Groups* Third Edition (Washington, DC: Government Printing Office, 1991); Elijah Saunders, ed., *Cardiovascular Diseases in African Americans* (Philadelphia, PA: F.A. Davis, 1991); Lawrence E. Gary and Bogart R. Leashore, "High Risk Status of Black Men," *Social Work* 27 (1982): 54-58; Lawrence E. Gary, ed., *Black Men* (Beverly Hills, CA: Sage, 1981), 21-71.

3. Ibid.

4. Barbara S. Dohrenwend, "Social Status and Stressful Life Events," *Journal of Personality and Social Psychology* 28 (1973):225-235; Alexander R. Askenasy, Bruce P. Dohrenwend, and Barbara S. Dohrenwend, "Some Effects of Social Class and Ethnic Group Membership on Judgements of the Magnitude of Stressful Life Events: A Research Note," *Journal Health and Social Behavior* 18 (1977): 432-439; Hector F. Myers, "Stress, Ethnicity, and Social Class: A Model for Research with Black Populations," in Enrico E. Jones and Sheldon J. Korchin, eds., *Minority Mental Health* (New York: Praeger, 1982), 118-148.

5. Myers, "Stress, Ethnicity, and Social Class."

6. Cary S. Kart, "Diversity Among Aged Black Males," in *Black Aged: Understanding Diversity and Service Needs*, ed. Zev Harel, Edward A. McKinney, and Michael Williams (Newbury Park, CA: Sage, 1990), 100-113.

7. Ibid.

8. Ibid.; Gary, *Black Men.*

9. Diane R. Brown and Lawrence E. Gary, "Stressful Life Events, Social Support Networks, and Physical and Mental Health of Urban Black Adults," *Journal of Human Stress* 13 (1987): 165-174; William W. Dressler and Lee W. Badger, "Epidemiology of Depressive Symptoms in Black Communities," *Journal of Nervous Disease* 173 (1985): 212-220; Thanh V. Tran, Roosevelt Wright, Jr, and Linda Chatters, "Health, Stress, Psychological Resources, and Subjective Well-Being Among Older Adults," *Psychology and Aging* 6 (1991): 100-108; Baqar A.Husaini, Stephen T. Moore, Robert S. Castor, William Neser, et al., "Social Density, Stressors, and Depression: Gender Differences Among the Black Elderly," *Journal of Gerontology: Psychological Sciences* 46 (1991): P236-242.

10. Dressler and Badger, "Epidemiology of Depressive Symptoms in Black Communities."

11. Brown and Gary, "Stressful Life Events, Social Support Networks, and Physical and Mental Health of Urban Black Adults."

12. Lawrence E. Gary, "Correlates of Depressive Symptoms Among a Select Population of Black Men," *American Journal of Public Health* 75 (1985): 1220-1222.

13. Thanh V. Tran, Roosevelt Wright, Jr, and Linda Chatters, "Health, Stress, Psychological Resources, and Subjective Well-Being Among Older Adults."

14. Thanh V. Tran, Roosevelt Wright, Jr, and Linda Chatters, "Health, Stress, Psychological Resources, and Subjective Well-Being Among Older Adults."

15. Baqar A.Husaini, Stephen T. Moore, Robert S. Castor, William Neser, et al., "Social Density, Stressors, and Depression: Gender Differences Among the Black Elderly."

16. Anita DeLongis, James C. Coyne, Gayle Dakof, Susan Folkman, and Richard S. Lazarus, "Relationship of Daily Hassles, Uplifts, and Major Life Events to Health," *Health Psychology* 1 (1982): 119-136; Carole K. Holahan, Charles J. Holahan, and Sharyn S. Belk, "Adjustment in Aging: The Roles of Life Stress, Hassles, and Self-Efficacy," *Health Psychology* 3 (1984): 315-328.

17. Lawrence E. Gary, Diane R. Brown, Norweeta G. Milburn, Feroz Ahmed, and Jacqueline Booth, *Depression in Black American Adults: Findings from the Norfolk Area Health Study* (Washington, DC: Institute for Urban Affairs and Research, Howard University, 1989).

18. Lenore S. Radloff, "The CES-D Scale: A Self-Report Depression Scale for Research in the General Population," *Applied Psychological Measurement* 3 (1977): 385-401.

19. Richard H. Rahe, "Epidemiological Studies of life change and illness," *International Journal of Psychiatry in Medicine* 6 (1975): 133-146.

20. Allen D. Kanner, James C. Coyne, Catherine Schafer, and Richard Lazarus, "Comparison of Two Modes of Stress Measurement: Daily Hassles and Uplifts Versus Major Life Events," *Journal of Behavioral Medicine* 4 (1981):1-39.

21. Fran Norris and Stanley A. Murrell, "Protective Function of Resources Related to Life Events, Global Stress, and Depression in Older Adults," *Journal of Health and Social Behavior* 25 (1984): 424-437.

22. Leonard Pearlin and Carmi Schooler, "The Structure of Coping," *Journal of Health and Social Behavior* 19 (1978): 2-21.

23. Manuel Barrera, Jr., Irwin N. Sandler, and Thomas B. Ramsay, "Preliminary Development of a Scale of Social Support: Studies on College students," *American Journal of Community Psychology* 9 (1981): 435-447.

24. Neal Krause and Kyriakos Markides, "Measuring Social Support Among Older Adults," *International Journal of Aging and Human Development* 30 (1990): 37-53.

25. Norris and Murrell, "Protective Function of Resources Related to Life Events, Global Stress, and Depression in Older Adults;" Lisa F. Berkman, Cathy S. Berkman, Stanislav Kasl, Daniel Freeman, Jr., et al., "Depressive Symptoms in Relation to Physical Health and Functioning in the Elderly," *American Journal of Epidemiology* 124 (1986): 372-388.

26. Berkman et al., "Depressive Symptoms in Relation to Physical Health and Functioning in the Elderly;" Stanley A. Murrell, Samuel Himmelfarb, and Katherine Wright, "Prevalence of Depression and Its Correlates in Older Adults," *American Journal of Epidemiology* 117 (1983): 173-185.

27. Asenath L. LaRue, Lew Bank, Lissy Jarvik, and Monte Hetland, "Health in Old Age: How do Physicians' ratings and self-ratings compare?," *Journal of Gerontology* 34 (1979): 687-691.

28. N. Bradburn, *The Structure of Psychological Well-Being* (Chicago: Aldine, 1969).

29. Lawrence E. Gary, et al., *Depression in Black American Adults: Findings from the Norfolk Area Health Study.*

30. Jacqueline M. Smith, "Function and Supportive Roles of Church," in *Aging in Black America*, James S. Jackson, Linda M. Chatters, and Robert J. Taylor (eds.) (Newbury Park, CA: Sage, 1993): 124-147.

31. Tran et al.,"Health, Stress, Psychological Resources, and Subjective Well-Being Among Older Adults;" Kyriakos S. Markides and David J. Lee, "Predictors of Health Status in Middle-Aged and Older Mexican Americans," *Journal of Gerontology: Social Sciences* 46 (1991): S243-249.

32. Markides and Lee, "Predictors of Health Status in Middle-Aged and Older Mexican Americans."

33. Husaini et al., "Social Density, Stressors, and Depression;" Brown and Gary, "Stressful Life Events, Social Support Networks, and Physical and Mental Health of Urban African American Adults."

The Gender Role and Contraceptive Attitudes of Young Men: Implications for Future African American Families

Bruce H. Wade

This research reports the contraceptive and gender role attitudes of a convenience sample of 60 working class African American youth enrolled in discussion groups in a clinical setting in Atlanta, Georgia. Most of the youth were close to both parents and received considerable parental support. They were *not*, as a group, rape-prone or in favor of abortion. The study found that only half of the youth received "enough" information about contraception from either parent. Forty-three percent felt that contraception was the female's responsibility and roughly 30 percent held strong anti-condom attitudes. The three most popular contraceptive techniques were the condom, pill and condom/pill. There was a significant difference in rating of the withdrawal technique between those whose fathers had provided enough contraceptive information and those whose fathers did not. An inverse correlation existed between rating of the pill and condom and rating of pregnancy as a positive event. Moreover, the more contraceptive information provided by the mother, the lower was the contraceptive attitudes score.

THEORETICAL CONTEXT

What does the future hold for the African American family? Without the cultural script which has guided our diverse ancestors, it is difficult to answer this question. Social forces in the United States have reeked havoc on American youth in general and on African American youth in particular. In order to begin making projections about this troubled generation, it is first necessary to scrutinize the attitudes and behaviors of African American adolescents. Their socially determined attitudes influence their relationships and preventative health care behaviors. Understanding attitudes is imperative for improved gender relations and for constructive reproductive behaviors.

A matrix of political, social, educational and economic crises imperil African American youth and families. Although many writers have attempted to indict the African American family system and culture as the cause of these problems, the truth is more complex.[1] The effects of the concurrent specters of AIDS, unwanted or early pregnancy, family disruption (including the avoidance of parental responsibility) and feminized poverty have created barriers to upward mobility. Sexually transmitted disease, unplanned pregnancy and family patterns are influenced by social structure and culture; each has implications for families. The main contributors to feminized poverty have been unemployment, poverty and divorce. In 1990, only 39.4 percent of African American children were living in two-parent households; the percentage among whites, by contrast, was 77.4 percent.[2] Moreover, the Bureau of the Census reports that:

> Compared with children living with two parents, children living with one parent are more likely to have a parent who has low income, and who is less educated, unemployed, and rents their home.[3]

Much of the social science literature has viewed African American cultural adaptations as dysfunctional and pathological.[4] Some African American researchers, however, have offered a less biased account.[5] Sullivan studied northeastern youth and found significant differences among the attitudes and practices of sexually active African American, white and Hispanic fathers.[6] Many African American adolescent fathers who were "officially absent," i.e., unmarried and non-supportive of their offspring, actually contributed to their child's social and economic support. Such behaviors are culturally induced but mediated by the social and political structures which hinder the parental contributions of the under-employed and the under-paid.

History and African American Gender Roles

African American gender roles are a consequence of history and social structure. Hill-Collins posits that the "Afrocentric ideology of motherhood" is a composite of African American cultural adaptations to slavery and oppression.[7] African American women were not protected from racial injustice, hence, ". . . the separate spheres of providing as a male domain and affective nurturing as a female domain did not develop within African-American families."[8] African American gender roles involve social support, community-based childcare, more egalitarian gender roles and informal adoption. Family structure, socioeconomic status[9] and social structure[10] influence contraceptive attitudes and gender roles.

The cumulative effects of socioeconomic status, urbanization, and family dynamics set the stage for the lives of youth.[11] It has been shown that adolescent childbearing runs in cycles and frequently endangers children's health and educational attainment.[12] These families have a high probability of remaining female-headed and dependent. Ninety percent of African American teenage parents (who have custody of their offspring) have never been married.[13] This study assesses the impact of parental involvement on sexual and contraceptive attitudes. The following questions were posed:

1. How do adolescent African American males feel about specific contraceptives and how do they define their contraceptive roles and responsibilities?

2. How do parents influence the contraceptive attitudes of their adolescent sons?

3. How do adolescent males interpret the concept of a sexual double standard?

4. How do adolescent males define their gender roles associated with their childrearing responsibilities?

METHODOLOGY

Sample

The convenience sample consisted of 60 working and middle-class adolescent males in an urban, clinical setting. The majority of the respondents were African American with the exception of two Hispanics. Most of those sampled were high school and junior high school students. Their ages ranged from 14 to 17 years with an average age of 16.

The respondents were contacted through "Teen Clinics" administered by county agencies in the Atlanta, Georgia Standard Metropolitan Statistical Area (SMSA). Males were referred to such clinics for sports physicals and outpatient health services. They were invited to attend periodic health-focused discussion groups. According to staff, very few males came to the clinics for contraceptive materials. Since the sample was not randomly selected, no attempt was made to generalize the findings to the entire Atlanta, Georgia SMSA.

Instrumentation

A questionnaire was constructed and administered by two trained Research Assistants and the Principal Investigator. The survey was pretested on a small group of African American male adolescents and revised to ensure that it was linguistically and culturally appropriate. The majority of the items utilized the 5-point Likert Scale format. Gender role attitudes were measured with items adapted from several published gender role scales. Reliable, additive rating scales were formed to assess global gender role and contraceptive attitudes. A Semantic Differential Scale was used to rank perceptions of particular contraceptive techniques, and items were developed which tapped related attitudes and self-reported behaviors. The data were analyzed using SPSS/PC software.

The confidentiality of the respondents was protected by instructing the respondents *not* to place their names on the instruments.

FINDINGS

Socioeconomic Status

The students in the sample were primarily of working and middle class backgrounds. Nearly half (46%) lived with both parents. It should be noted that this figure is significantly higher than the overall percentage of African American two-parent households as reported in the 1990 census. Of the mothers whose occupations were reported, 35 percent were unemployed, 28 percent held "blue collar" jobs, 7 percent were white collar workers, and 16 percent were "professionals" at the time of the survey; (14 percent were unknown). Among the fathers, 12 percent were unemployed, 43 percent held blue collar jobs, 16 percent held white collar jobs and 5 percent were professionals. A revealing 24 percent of the respondents did not know their father's occupation.

Sixty nine percent of the males surveyed planned to attend college, 16 percent aspired to blue collar occupations and 15 percent did not know their educational goals beyond high school. In light of the recent performance of African American males in the educational system, the high proportion of college aspirants reflect either a very optimistic outlook or a sample skewed toward middle class goals. Seventy seven percent of the respondents believed that it was *not* difficult for young men like them to get a "good" job.

General Sexual Attitudes

While most (78.1%) of the students surveyed felt that young people should plan when and where they have sexual intercourse, 59 percent did not require being "in love" to engage in coitus. Sixty one percent agreed that if they fathered a child, it would be their responsibility to support the child financially and socially.

Poverty-related Attitudes

The literature on the so called "subculture of poverty" suggests that groups which are prone to poverty have different "values" and attitudes from the middle class. Some researchers speculate that the overemphasis on toughness among males interferes with upward mobility.[14] In this sample, 83 percent of the respondents believed that "it is very important for a man to be tough in life." This fact in isolation does not indicate an "over emphasis" nor does it necessarily generate self-destructive behavior.

Proponents of the culture of poverty thesis also claim that the sexual objectification of women is correlated with ethnicity and low socioeconomic status. The majority of the respondents (80%) agreed with the statement that they respect young men who have lots of girlfriends. Nevertheless, this attitude did not correspond with a propensity for sexual violence. Only 9 percent agreed that it was "sometimes OK for a man to force a woman to have sex."

Family Structure and Cohesiveness

Eighty two percent of the students reported being "very close" to their mothers, and over half (59%) reported being close to their fathers. This is evidence that the majority of the students in this sample were strongly influenced by their mothers. They also had close bonds with their fathers in spite of the fact that a slight majority did not live with both parents.

Although not the most intimate means of family interaction, television viewing is one of the most common family activities in America. The average amount of time respondents reported spending watching television amounted to two to four hours per day. While it is not the focus of this study, television is widely acknowledged as influencing attitudes and behavior. One indirect measure of family cohesiveness in this study, therefore, was whether or not the respondents were aware of their parents' favorite television show. Half (50%) of the students knew their mother's favorite television show and only 35 percent knew their father's favorite program. More than one-quarter (26.7%) of the respondents reported that they had no significant role models in their lives. Among those who were able to identify role models, 16 percent cited their fathers (primarily those whose fathers held white collar occupations), and 12 percent selected basketball stars.

Attitudes Towards Contraception and Condoms

Forty seven percent of the respondents agreed with the statement that "most birth control is not healthy for girls to use." Fourteen percent felt that pregnancy prevention was not possible. On the whole, condoms were rated by this group as the most effective contraceptive device. However, there were anti-condom attitudes expressed by approximately one-in-four respondents. Twenty nine percent of them felt that using condoms made sex less enjoyable; 28 percent felt too embarrassed to purchase condoms from a local drugstore and 24 percent agreed with the statement that they should use condoms only if they think a girl is "nasty." Moreover, 18 percent reported that if they were in love, they would *not* use a condom, and 11 percent indicated that hiding condoms from parents was difficult. Only 9 percent of the respondents, however, complained about the high cost of condoms.

Contraception and Gender Role Scales

Scales were devised to assess attitudes concerning contraceptive and gender roles. The Contraceptive Attitudes Scale included 5 items with a Cronbach's Alpha reliability coefficient of .74. The gender role scale was composed of 4 items with a Cronbach's Alpha reliability coefficient of .67. Thus, there was reasonably high internal consistency in the scales.

Research question 1. The semantic differential was used to ascertain youth opinions toward particular methods of birth control. Based on the mean responses to each technique [with 4 symbolizing "the best" technique and 1 symbolizing "the worst], the techniques were subjectively ranked as follows: condoms, birth control pills, condom & pill, condom & spermicide, withdrawal, diaphragm, rhythm, spermicide, and abortion.

The orientation toward contraception was also assessed. The primary means of rating these attitudes was the contraceptive attitudes scale. The scale items measured general attitudes toward obtaining and using contraceptives. The higher the scale score, the more positive the orientation towards contraception. The range of scores on this scale was from 9 to 17 and the highest possible score was 20. The mean scale score for contraceptive attitudes was 10.98, the median and the mode were roughly the same (11) and the standard deviation was 2.98.

The general attitude toward contraceptive responsibility was ambivalent. Forty four percent claimed that using contraceptives was a young woman's responsibility and the majority scored near the mean on the Contraceptive Attitudes Scale; i.e., most retained indefinite ideas about contraception. Only one third (35%) scored *above* the mean. The most approved technique was the condom and the least approved was abortion (see Table 1).

Research question 2 examined the linkage between contraceptive attitudes of parents and those of their sons. The amount of information about contraception provided by the mother was inversely correlated ($r = -.273$, $p = .05$) with the contraceptive attitudes rating.

The *t* Test indicated that there was a significant difference between males who received sufficient information from fathers (vs. those who did not) in the orientation towards the withdrawal technique. Youth who indicated that their fathers had provided them with "enough" information regarding "birth control," were significantly more favorable towards coitus interruptus.

There were no significant associations between the closeness to either parent and the overall contraceptive attitudes scale, nor between the amount of contraceptive information provided by the mother and the rating of any specific technique.

TABLE 1
Ranking of Contraceptive Methods by Respondents

Contraceptive Method	Mean Score	Standard Deviation
Condoms	4.1	2.3
Birth Control Pills	3.9	2.6
Condom and Pills	3.6	3.2
Withdrawal	3.6	2.9
Diaphragm	3.0	3.3
Rhythm	2.9	3.4
Foam	2.0	2.6
Abortion	1.6	.94

Research question 3 examined the attitudes towards the sexual double standard. Although the attitudes of the sample were relatively gender egalitarian, a sexual double standard was prevalent. Only 6.9 percent agreed that "it's OK for girls to have more than one boyfriend at a time," yet 19.7 percent felt that it was OK for males to have multiple girlfriends.

Research question 4 assessed the gender role and parenting attitudes of young males. The scale scores ranged from 6 to 11. The gender role attitude scale consisted of four items with a mean of 7.0, a median of 7.0, a mode of 5.0; the standard deviation was 2.26.

The overall interpretation of gender roles was somewhat egalitarian in this sample. Higher scores indicate relatively traditional gender role attitudes and low scores indicate egalitarian attitudes. Sixty three percent of the respondents scored at or below the mean value for this scale. Surprisingly, respondents who were closest to their fathers were more likely to have egalitarian gender role attitudes ($r = -.279$, $p = .048$).

"Traditional" or less egalitarian males were more likely to feel that males should pay child support even if a woman became pregnant intentionally ($r = .292$, $p = .040$). They were also most likely to favor males having multiple girlfriends.

Most of the young men surveyed were against "early pregnancy," possibly due to their college aspirations. Moreover, sixty seven percent disagreed that "getting a girl pregnant should make a young man proud and happy." There was a strong correlation, however, between agreement with this statement and agreement with the idea that having many girlfriends was something positive ($r = .446$, $p = .001$), indicating that those with "hypersexual" attitudes were the most likely to look favorably on pregnancy.

A significant association was found between "pronatal" (favoring pregnancy) values and contraceptive preference. Youth who professed pronatal values were more likely to have negative views about birth control pills ($r = -.458$, $p = .002$) and the combination technique of condoms & spermicide ($r = -.332$, $p = .028$) i.e., the most effective forms of contraception. This suggests conflicting ethics between the value of having children and the concept of contraception.

Taking responsibility for children is a process quite distinct from conception. The split between youth who felt that "it is *always* the man's job to support his children" (49%) and those who disagreed with the statement (51%) was about even. Only 17 percent felt that young men should *not* have to pay child support if conception was part of a plot to entrap them. Forty four percent agreed with the idea that "(I)t is better for a girl my age to have a baby rather than get an abortion."

The correlation analysis showed that "traditional" males were less likely to attend church ($r = -.271$, $p = .05$) and less likely to hold attitudes conducive to the use of birth control pills ($r = -.290$, $p = .05$).

An astounding indication of the influence of maternal heads of household was the finding that males whose mothers had provided them with "enough" contraceptive information were more likely to feel that it was "OK for young women to have multiple boyfriends" ($r = .397$, $p = .003$).

CONCLUSIONS

While culture is not a cause of the problems faced by African American families, it can (and should) be used as a means to help alleviate the massive strains within and among them. In light of the hyperbole and hysteria surrounding urban male youth and their projected demise, this analysis leaves room for both hope and concern. The hope is that young men will be nurtured, encouraged and motivated to pursue their individual and social goals; i.e., self-actualization, college attendance, and fathering children socially *and* biologically. They should also be taught the value of collective responsibility to their ethnic group. Adult males also help to socialize their young counterparts regardless of family ties.

The concern is that, in the absence of suitable guidance, youth such as these will succumb to the more perverse forces in this society which propel young African American men toward early parenthood, morbidity, violence, incarceration, and even death. Both our culture and our expertise can enable future generations to thrive in America. African Americans must take advantage of linkages within the Diaspora to create their own means of production and employment. In this way, African American men will be in a better position to act as role models for African American children. African American youth require gender-specific interventions which will benefit both themselves and society. Sex education and disease prevention are areas that African American professionals in public health, medicine, education and related disciplines must address. African Americans who have already succeeded have a responsibility in this society to help pave the way for all of *our* children, in culturally appropriate ways. If we do not, no one will!

The attitudes reflected in this study demonstrate that most of these young men are responsible. They care what happens to their offspring and to their mates, and most approach sexual encounters rationally. In lieu of supportive fathers or traditional secret societies and other social institutions geared toward the development of African American men, youth require knowledge of their distant and immediate ancestors. Factual information must be presented to both adolescent males and to their parents in order to counteract the misinformation and stereotypical attitudes which promote unhealthy lifestyles.

In this study, findings concerning parental contributions to sex education were troubling. The study found that the attitude of respondents toward withdrawal was most favorable in cases where the fathers played a sufficient role in the sexual education of their sons. This traditional technique does not protect young men from AIDS and it is also ineffective as a means of contraception. Fathers must be educated along with sons and daughters regarding the dangers of AIDS and ineffective birth control. Since the cultural value of procreation may counteract the information regarding the most effective forms of contraception and disease prevention, youth and adults must come together to discuss meaningful ways to deal with both issues.

This survey found that youth were closer to their fathers than most of the literature suggests and that fathers helped convey egalitarian gender role attitudes to their sons. Only one third of the participants, however, reported that they had a male role model in their lives. Moreover, those who did name a role model identified with sports figures nearly as often as they identified with their own fathers. This finding suggests that the use of sports figures in sex education may be a worthy enterprise. Fathers and other men must transmit appropriate knowledge to youth so that they may develop their sense of family and community responsibility.

The inverse association between the quantity of contraceptive information provided by the mother and the scores on the contraceptive attitudes scale suggests that *some* mothers may not impart sufficient contraceptive information to their sons. The greater the amount of information provided by the mother, the lower was the contraceptive attitude score. This low level of commitment to contraception may be associated with the exhortations of abstinence through scare tactics (threats of HIV infection or unwanted pregnancy). The mixed message young African American men receive regarding the simplistic dichotomy of "good" and "bad" women may also contribute to this finding. Many parents do not provide enough specific information to adolescents who, in the heat of passion, neglect to protect themselves. Consequently, both parents must be more involved in the sexual education of their sons, so that accurate information is provided to counteract misinformation and mixed messages received from other sources. Furthermore, it may be that some mothers are disenchanted with *adult* male sexual attitudes and behaviors, and these attitudes may be transferred to sons in ways that interfere with responsible behavior.

While culture is not at the root of the problem, some cultural attitudes may be self-defeating. The misogynist view of women (championed in some rap music) indicates that part of the problem of non-supportive fathers appears as a consequence of poverty-induced attitudes. A sizable proportion of this sample emphasized physical toughness, hypersexual attitudes (having many girlfriends), and traditional gender attitudes which discourage contraceptive attempts. This trend must be counteracted primarily by responsible African American people.

Pronatal attitudes are a part of American and African American culture. Positive attitudes toward pregnancy were relatively common in this sample and attitudes towards abortion were relatively adverse (44 percent favored pregnancy over abortion if given the choice). These attitudes become problematic when parents can not or do not support their children. The future of the family depends on the dedication and sacrifice of politically conscious adults.

NOTES

Special thanks to Teresa Leary and Donald Tunnage for their assistance in the data collection.

1. Daniel P. Moynihan, *The Negro Family: The Case for National Action* (U.S. Department of Labor: Washington, D.C., 1965); Elliott Liebow, *Tally's Corner* (Boston: Little, Brown, 1967).

2. U.S. Bureau of the Census, "Household and Family Characteristics: March 1990 & 1989," *Current Population Reports*, Series P-29, No. 447 (Washington, DC: Government Printing Office, 1990).

3. U.S. Bureau of the Census, "Marital Status and Living Arrangements: March 1989," *Current Population Reports*, Series P- 20, No. 445 (Washington, DC: Government Printing Office, 1990).

4. Moynihan, *The Negro Family.*

5. Joyce Ladner, *Tomorrow's Tomorrow: The Black Woman* (Garden City, NJ: Anchor Books, 1972); J. Taylor Gibbs (ed.), *Young, Black and Male in America: An Endangered Species* (Dover: Auburn House, 1988).

6. Mercer L. Sullivan, "Absent Fathers in the Inner City," *The Annals of the American Academy of Political and Social Science* 501 (January, 1989).

7. Patricia Hill Collins, "The Meaning of Motherhood in Black Culture," *SAGE: A Scholarly Journal on Black Women* (Fall, 1987).

8. Ibid., 7.

9. Kristen Luker, "Dubious Conceptions: The Controversy over teen pregnancy," *The American Prospect* (Spring, 1991).

10. William J. Wilson, *The Truly Disadvantaged: The Inner City, the Underclass, and Public Policy* (Chicago: The University of Chicago Press, 1987).

11. Dennis P. Hogan and Evelyn M. Kitagawa, "The Impact of Social Status, Family Structure, and Neighborhood on the Fertility of Black Adolescents," *American Journal of Sociology* 90 (1985): 825–855.

12. Alva P. Barnett, "Sociocultural Influences on Adolescent Mothers." In *The Black Family: Essays and Studies*, Robert Staples (ed.) (Belmont: Wadsworth 1986).

13. U.S. Bureau of the Census, "Marital Status and Living Arrangements."

14. Walter Miller, "Lower Class Culture as a Generating Milieu of Gang Delinquency," *Journal of Social Issues* 14 (1958).

Urban Adolescent Homicidal Violence: An Emerging Public Health Concern

Ronald K. Barrett

Homicidal violence among adolescent youth in American inner cities has been documented and studied for some time. A pattern of elevated lethal violence has been observed to peak during adolescence; this has resulted in homicide being identified as one of the major causes of death among adolescents. Further, homicide is reported to be particularly prevalent among ethnic minority males residing in major metropolitan areas in the United States. Even more alarming is the fact that the perpetrators of these homicides are also adolescent urban youth. The reality of this pattern of homicidal violence among urban adolescent youth begs more thorough conceptual study.

The pattern of homicidal violence among urban adolescent youth, particularly African Americans is cause for grave concern. This article critically examines: (1) the nature and scope of the pattern of lethal violence among adolescent urban youth; (2) theoretical explanations of homicidal violence, and (3) implications for community involvement and intervention.

THE NATURE AND SCOPE OF ADOLESCENT HOMICIDAL VIOLENCE

More than half of all serious crimes in the United States (murder, rape, aggravated assault, robbery, burglary, larceny, and motor vehicle theft) are committed by youth aged 10 to 17.[1] Between 1960 and 1980, juvenile crime rose twice as fast as adult crime. In Northern California, children 17 and under are arrested for 57 percent of all felonies against people (homicide, assault, rape, etc.) and for 66 percent of property crime. In Chicago, one third of all murders were committed by persons aged 20 or younger—a 29 percent jump over 1975.[2] A study of homicides in Los Angeles during 1988 revealed that victims were most frequently between the ages of 15 and 24, and were primarily African American and Hispanic males.[3] In addition, the perpetrators of homicidal violence were also primarily in this age group.

The dramatic increase in the level of lethal violence among youth has been reflected by a consistent increase in the number of violent crimes reported in American urban areas over the last three decades.[4] Violent crimes attributed to African American adolescents has significantly impacted the life expectancy for African Americans, making felony homicide the leading cause of death among African Americans.[5] The significant level of elevated violence is sufficient cause for homicide not to be viewed as merely a criminal justice issue, but rather as an urgent public health concern.[6]

A study conducted by the National Center for Health Statistics reported the United States homicide rate to be up to 70 times the homicide rate in other countries. Moreover, three-fourths of these homicides were committed with firearms, compared with less than one-fourth in the other countries. This report also emphasized a concern about the increase in firearm mortality among children and youth.[7] Another study conducted by the National Center for Health Statistics reveals an alarming pattern of escalating lethal violence between 1979 and 1988 among children and young adults. In 1988, 77 percent of homicides among teenagers 15 to 19 years of age were associated with firearm use; the rate was 88 percent among African American males. Among 20- to 24-year-olds, 70 percent of homicides resulted from firearm use; the rate was 81 percent among African American males. Among 25- to 29-year-olds, 68 percent of homicides were firearm related; the rate was 75 percent among African American males. Among 30- to 34-year olds, 64 percent of the homicides resulted from firearm use; the rate was 70 percent among African American males.[8]

What are the factors related to this violent trend among youth? What are the social and psychological bases for such violence? The next section presents a discussion of a number of theoretical perspectives on this issue.

THEORETICAL EXPLANATIONS OF ADOLESCENT VIOLENCE

Winbush observes that theories of criminal behavior among youth are as varied as those who offer them.[9] The crimes youth commit appear to be a function of economic, political, racial, or sex role values. Thus, any attempt to articulate a comprehensive theoretical explanation of adolescent violence is problematic due to the ubiquitous and varied situational context in which these behaviors occur. However, the prevailing theoretical points of view do offer useful insights into the nature of this pervasive and complex phenomenon.

Economic Deprivation Thesis

Robert Merton, a conservative sociologist, has developed the capitalist theoretical view that crime among youth in America is an understandable consequence of the pursuit of status, recognition, and esteem through the acquisition of the material goods associated with success and prosperity.[10] The assumptions of this view, however, have been challenged by Title et al. in a review of 35 studies of juvenile delinquents.[11] Their review found a significant decline in the relationship between crime and social class over the past 40 years. Nonetheless, social class has been significantly correlated with the incidence of violent crimes. That is, poorer individuals are more likely to commit violent crimes against persons, while affluent individuals are more likely to commit white-collar crimes. Property crimes, however, have not been linked to social class.

While the Economic Deprivation Thesis seems reasonable, its position is weakened by the observation of violence among middle-class ethnic minority youth. It is more plausible that socioeconomic status impacts a variety of factors that may indirectly influence the pattern of homicidal violence observed. Many researchers attribute some significance to poverty, unemployment, and racism on the level of violent crimes in American society.[12] The relationship between these conditions and homicidal violence is complex and worthy of further study.

Subculture of Violence Thesis

According to the sociological thesis of Wolfgang and Ferracuti, the overrepresentation of assaultive violence among African Americans may be attributed to the unique ecological dynamics of ghetto life and a subculture that models and sanctions violence as a way of life.[13] Implicit in this thesis is the belief that certain sociological groups are more prone to violence because it is sanctioned by the subculture they inhabit. African American scholars critical of the subculture of violence thesis stress the importance of viewing urban violence in the proper socioeconomic and cultural context.[14] Other scholars reject the thesis, deeming it overly simplistic.[15]

Curtis builds on the thesis of the African American culture of poverty and provides a "multidimensional value space" model that accounts for the important interaction of race, culture, poverty, and violence in urban settings.[16] Other critics argue that the subculture of violence tradition underestimates (if not ignores) the impact of the legacy of slavery and racism on the etiology of African American crime today.[17] Still others argue that the propensity for violence is not part of the cultural heritage African American's brought from Africa.[18] In their opinion, the study of criminology ought to involve a critical understanding of the larger society and the cultural context in which the behavior occurs. Indeed, Staples views African American homicide as "normative" not because of a unique African American subculture of violence, but rather because it is a fundamental aspect of the larger pattern of American culture, particularly its historical and traditional styles of relating to ethnic minorities.[19] Consequently, to view and characterize this behavior as a socio-pathological component of the African American cultural experience is an exercise in victim blaming. A consideration of the cultural, socioeconomic, and political influences, as well as the historical legacy of slavery and racism in their varied forms and manifestations, is essential for understanding the etiology of African American homicidal violence.

According to the thesis, one would expect all members of the socially disadvantaged subculture to be violent in response to their condition. Thus, findings that show a discrepant pattern in the incidence of expressed lethal violence among ethnic minority women further discredits the thesis. For example, findings from studies of homicide by race and sex suggest that in comparison to other groups, African American females are more likely to be victims of homicide, are more likely to be victimized in the home, and are less likely to be "primary offenders" and accomplices.[20]

The concept of an existing subculture that supports and nurtures violence needs to be explored in greater depth. Particular emphasis should be placed on the social and ecological variables that manifest this behavior in a "male subculture of violence." Empirical findings that homicidal violence is generally a male-dominated expression of criminal behavior is worthy of further investigative study.

The Psychoanalytic Thesis

According to this view, the high incidence of violence among African Americans and Hispanics may be a function of "poorly developed" mechanisms for coping with the anger and rage caused by situations of economic deprivation, poverty, and discrimination.[21] The combination of unsublimated anger and low impulse control coupled with the easy availability of handguns and easy victims (i.e., other African Americans) creates potentially violent situations for countless African Americans. According to this view, the high incidence of "Black-on-Black" homicide reflects a process of displacement of affect on the part of African Americans who have low self-esteem and high levels of hostility and frustration in response to their limited social and economic possibilities.[22] Grier and Cobb argue that the chronic and severe frustrations that African American males experience in American society may engender understandable levels of frustration, rage, and aggression.[23] These emotions, in turn, are displaced onto victims of convenience in their immediate environment.[24]

The Psychoanalytic Thesis of criminal behavior also considers the socialization process involved in producing the "socialized criminal."[25] That is, if one's social environment condones or is supportive of violent criminal behavior, an individual can be socialized to commit violent crimes. This approach contends that people exposed more to antisocial influences than to law-conforming influences may reflect this in their personalities and modes of interpersonal behavior.[26] Barrett offers a similar view in his interpretation of African American male homicidal and suicidal patterns in Los Angeles.[27] A major drawback to psychoanalytic research, however, is that it cannot be easily tested empirically. The hypothetical construct of personality cannot be observed and is difficult to measure. These measurement problems present methodological challenges for researchers interested in rigorously exploring psychoanalytic theories of violent criminal behavior.

The Social-Psychological Thesis

Criminal violent behavior among urban youth may be easily modeled, learned, and sanctioned during a developmental period when many adolescent youth struggle to achieve individuation and identity, and typically seek counter-culture expressions. This notion appears regularly in the theorizing about rebellious youth who become juvenile delinquents. Conformity and peer pressure of gangs and "posses" appear to be significant in explaining violent behavior among urban youth. The social environmental pressure and apparent attraction are visibly evident in the counter-culture of heavy metal and rap music, and in other forms of self-expression, including dress.[28]

Alcohol and drugs play a significant role in criminal behavior.[29] Gary reported that more African American males between 15 and 30 are victims of alcohol-related homicides than any other race-sex-age group.[30] Drug abuse among African American youth has increased over the past 25 years, spreading from the inner cities to the suburbs, and has become increasingly linked to "hard drugs" (i.e., heroin and crack cocaine) which are inextricably tied to violent street crime.[31] Alcohol and drugs are associated with the three major causes of death among African American males (i.e., homicide, suicide, and accidental deaths) as they lower inhibitions and increase feelings of frustration, often resulting in aggression. In addition, situational risk of acquisition, use and sale of drugs and alcohol are highly correlated with the increasing incidence of lethal violence.

The Dysfunctional Systems Thesis

A growing body of evidence suggests that at risk youth are products of family and educational systems that have failed them.[32] As a consequence, many of these youth reject the majority culture choosing alternative survival strategies for social esteem. Their behavior becomes a function of rewards acquired through conformity to in-group standards and values.[33]

In a study of a sample of 1,956 delinquent adolescents, Busch and colleagues found that adolescents who kill have certain characteristics, including criminally violent family members, gang membership, severe educational difficulties, and alcohol/drug abuse.[34] These findings have been documented by other researchers.[35] The dysfunctional systems thesis is consistent with numerous observational studies that correlate juvenile delinquency with failure in educational and other social institutions.

The Declining Value of Nonwhite Life Thesis

This thesis posits that youth have been socialized to value the life and welfare of whites more than that of nonwhites. As a consequence, the probability of urban minority youth victimizing members of their own reference group is increased. The theorized hierarchy of homicide offenses significantly impacts on "Black-on-Black" crime and explains the curious pattern of elevated homicidal violence among African Americans and other ethnic minorities in urban America.[36]

The "Declining Value of Nonwhite Life Thesis" is supported by a growing body of empirical evidence documenting that crimes involving both nonwhite victims and perpetrators are responded to differently by the criminal justice system. This difference needs to be the subject of further study in order to impact social policy aimed at reducing the level of lethal violence in the African American community, ultimately addressing the escalating violence that has become a public health concern for all African Americans.

In summary, the research on the influences of homicidal violence among urban adolescents has developed from a variety of theoretical frameworks. All of the explanations presented have some value and provide insight into the complex phenomenon of urban adolescent homicidal violence. No one explanation is adequate to fully account for and explain the various dimensions and scope of this phenomenon. Without exception all are worthy of additional empirical study. With few exceptions, better data gathering and management techniques are needed in order to develop descriptive causal models that will ultimately guide intervention strategies and impact social policy.

RECOMMENDATIONS FOR INTERVENTION AND SOCIAL POLICY IMPLICATIONS

Intervention needs to take place on a number of levels, primarily through community involvement. It is important that African Americans and other urban ethnic groups recognize the extent of the homicidal violence problem within their communities and develop a clear and unified strategy to address it. In neighborhoods where youthful gang violence is not only life-threatening to young African American and Hispanic males but also to the community at large, this criminal behavior must be labeled clearly unacceptable and should not be tolerated. Giving voice to such a protest must be coupled with a collective commitment to social action, social change, and multi-leveled intervention.

Community Empowerment

The African American church has historically been a major institutional resource in the struggles of African Americans. African American churches can provide essential leadership in many areas and can serve as a viable platform for educational campaigns and socialization efforts designed to discourage the transmission of values such as brutality and violence. In many instances, the family and domestic environment are an important initial point in intervention attempts to reduce social violence.[37]

Within the African American community, African American males must assume some responsibility for the insidious progression of criminal violence. In doing so, they must serve as leaders in regaining control of African American communities. The posture of finding fault for this dilemma solely outside of the African American community psychologically lessens the chances that African Americans will ever feel empowered to initiate the changes necessary within their community. The same is true for other ethnic groups. Others have no vested interest and cannot be depended upon to resolve a social and public health crisis that particularly victimizes young African American males, making them "an endangered species."[38]

There is a growing national grassroots movement among African American males to reclaim the inner cities and develop innovative social and community programs to serve younger African American males. There is a real need for programs in virtually every segment of the community (i.e., home, school, church, social clubs, athletics, entertainment, and so forth) to establish an "African American male agenda—nurturing and cultivating future leadership." While the assistance and support of caring and committed females is necessary and valued, the primary leadership and impetus must come from caring and committed older African American males. These men must serve as mentors to younger African American males, many of whom are victims of a complex array of social and environmental conditions that place them at perilous risk of self-destruction and lethal violence.

While there is a crucial need to hold educational institutions more accountable for the personal and professional development of African American and Hispanic youth, especially males, there is critical need for a "survival education and socialization agenda." At every level in the educational process, the evidence is clear that when parents show interest, children are more likely to succeed. The level of apathy and passive involvement among African American and Hispanic parents must change. African American and Hispanic fathers (as well as mothers) must become actively involved and not entrust the education and socialization of their children to others.

Historically, educational institutions, which lack a vested interest in and appreciation of African American and Hispanic youth, have failed them miserably and have, more often than not, blamed them for their plight. As argued by contemporary African

American visionaries, alternative educational and socialization systems are necessary for the development and salvaging of young African American and other nonwhite males.[39] A crucial part of this educational and socialization agenda should address Afrocentric and Hispanic cultural values, self-esteem enhancement, drug and sex education, a sense of community and collective accountability, and political and social strategies for survival in a multicultural and racist environment that is often hostile to their well being.

Given the reality and probability of lethal confrontations for younger African American and Hispanic males, it is imperative to systematically educate them about the risks of lethal confrontations and help them develop skills for managing these situations. For example, if, as available research data suggest, there is a real risk of homicide associated with robbery, then developing skills in lethal confrontations is in order. Further, if given a choice in a robbery, young African American and Hispanic males should be instructed to choose life over the value of material possessions or "saving face." In addition, self-defense and conflict management skills may hold some promise for reducing the incidence of homicidal violence among young African American and Hispanic males.

Lethal confrontations with peace and law enforcement officers should be realistically regarded as situations of risk for *all* nonwhite young males. Developing an awareness of these encounters as situations of potential risk, knowledge of police and peace officer confrontation management skills, and knowledge of legal rights for recourse is a worthy agenda in assuring the well-being of young nonwhite males.

Criminal Justice Reform

There is an urgent need for community empowerment and a collective effort to address the inequities and discriminatory practices in the criminal justice system that excuse "Black-on- Black" criminal behavior and consequently encourage the propagation of homicidal violence in the African American and Hispanic community. Moreover, the laws and the operation of the criminal justice system need to be more equitable, not just in theory, but also in practice. While there is a need to correct the over-victimization of African American and Hispanic males within the various components of the criminal justice system, there is also a need to hold African American and Hispanic criminals more accountable, particularly when other African Americans and Hispanics are victims.

On a broader level, it is necessary to make correctional programs more operational in rehabilitation and counseling young ethnic minority males who are involved in criminal activity. Acknowledging the need for social and system change, we must also recognize that unless we begin to take some responsible action to impact the level of criminal violence, our future looks bleak.

On a societal level, the problem of socioeconomic inequities must be addressed. Indeed, such inequities create conditions of poverty and social stress that place the poor and underprivileged at greater risk of criminal violence. Social policies that do not address issues of inequity cannot reduce crime. Unemployment and economic inequality lead to crime only when they occur within a cultural context which infuses their victims with an acute sense of failure and rejection, which, in turn, produces a sense of "relative deprivation" and "thwarted ambition." In many instances, unskilled and unemployable ethnic minorities in urban America are being excluded from the legitimate economy. All too often, increasing numbers of younger people are finding a window of opportunity in the illegitimate economy at an astronomical cost to themselves and the local communities in which they reside.[40]

In addition, there is a serious need for policy changes at a federal level to lawfully ban the easy access and availability of automatic assault weapons. Such a ban could help curb the level of lethal violence in American urban areas, especially where gang-related violence and indiscriminant use of these weapons results in increased deaths and injury to growing numbers of victims annually. The laws should hold equal penalties for the possession and sale of these lethal instruments. Along with these policy changes, social and community efforts that offer amnesty to individuals encouraging them to surrender their weapons are a worthy undertaking.

Finally, there is a desperate need to develop, refine, and implement effective models of counseling and clinical intervention when working with victims and offenders of brutal and violent crimes. New theoretical models and therapeutic interventions are needed for work with populations that have special needs related to ethnicity, age, gender, and social class. The ultimate goal of psychological counseling should be to assist individuals with insight into their behavior, maximize their coping skills, and explore more socially acceptable coping mechanisms.

Attempts at curbing violence within the African American and Hispanic communities will be futile if the American "culture of violence" is not addressed.[41] Ultimately, there is a need to examine violence and acts of brutality as issues at a national and societal level. A critical examination of the conditions and societal influences that nurture violence as a way of life is worthy of further study. With these insights, informed interventions during rehabilitation and remediation are realizable. Our greatest hope for the future, however, is in *prevention*. As we approach the year 2000, we should examine the destructive consequences of a primitive and maladaptive way of being that nurtures violence and ultimately threatens the quality of life and existence of human kind.

NOTES

1. Raymond Winbush, "Growing Pains: Explaining Adolescent Violence with Developmental Theory," In J. Carlson and J. Lewis (eds.), *Counseling the Adolescent*, 57–73 (Denver, CO: Love Publishing Company, 1988).

2. U.S. Department of Justice, Federal Bureau of Investigation, *Uniform Crime Reports, Crime in the United States* (Washington, DC: Government Printing Office, 1990).

3. Ronald K. Barrett, "Homicide and Suicide: Who is At Risk?" *The American Black Male* (New York: William Pruitt Enterprises, 1991).

4. Harold M. Rose and Paula D. McClain (eds.) *Race, Place and Risk* (New York: State University Press, 1990); Darnell F. Hawkins (ed.) *Homicide among Black Americans.* (Lanham, MD: University Press of America, 1986).

5. Patrick O. O'Carroll and James Mercy, "Recent Trends in Black Homicide," In D. Hawkins (ed.) *Homicide Among Black Americans,* 29–42; Rose and McClain, *Race, Place and Risk;* Barrett, "Homicide and Suicide."

6. Ruth E. Dennis, "Social Stress and Mortality Among Non-white Males," *Phylon* 38 (1977): 315–328; Centers for Disease Control, "Homicide Among Young Black Males: United States, 1970–1982," *Morbidity Mortality Weekly Reports,* 34 (1985): 629–633; W. Rodney Hammond and Betty R. Yung, "Preventing Violence in At-risk African-American Youth," *Journal of Health Care for the Poor and Undeserved* 2(3) (1991): 359–373.

7. National Center for Health Statistics, "Advance Report of Final Mortality Statistics, 1988," *Monthly Vital Statistics Report* 39 (7) (1990), Hyattsville, Maryland: Public Health Service.

8. National Center for Health Statistics, "Firearm Mortality among Children, Youth, and Young Adults 1–34 Years of Age; Trends and Current Status: United States, 1979–88," *Monthly Vital Statistics Report* 39 (11) (1991), Hyattsville, MD: Public Health Services.

9. Winbush, "Growing Pains."

10. R. Merton, *Social Theory and Social Structure* (Glencoe, IL: Free Press, 1952).

11. C.R. Title, W.J. Villemez, & D.A. Smith, "The Myth of Social Class and Criminality," *American Social Review* 43 (1978): 643–656.

12. Walter B. Miller, "Lower Class Culture as a Generating Milieu of Gang Delinquency," *Journal of Social Issues* 14 (1938): 5-19; Carolyn R. Block, *Homicide in Chicago* (Chicago, IL: Center for Urban Policy, 1986); Winbush, "Growing Pains."

13. Marvin E. Wolfgang and Franco Ferracuti, *The Subculture of Violence* (Beverly Hills: Sage Publications, 1967).

14. Robert Staples, "Race and Family Violence: The Internal Colonialism Perspective." (Unpublished manuscript, 1976); Hawkins, *Homicide Among Black Americans*; Rose and McClain, *Race, Place and Risk.*

15. L. Curtis, *Violence, Race and Culture* (Lexington, MA: Lexington Books, 1975); Rose and McClain, *Race, Place and Risk.*

16. Curtis, *Violence, Race and Culture.*

17. Hawkins, *Homicide Among Black Americans.*

18. Paul Bohannon, (ed.) *African Homicide and Suicide* (Princeton, NJ: Princeton University Press, 1960); C. Silberman, *Criminal Violence-Criminal Justice: Criminals, Police, Courts, and Prisons in America* (New York: Random House, 1978).

19. Staples, "Race and Family Violence."

20. Block, *Homicide in Chicago;* O'Carroll and Mercy, "Recent Trends in Black Homicide."

21. Frantz Fanon, *The Wretched of the Earth* (New York: Grove Press, 1968); Fanon, *Black Skin, White Masks* (New York: Grove Press, 1967).

22. Alvin F. Poussaint, "Black on Black Homicide: A Psychological-Political Perspective," *Victimology* 8 (1983): 161-169.

23. William H. Grier and Price M. Cobbs, *Black Rage* (New York: Basic Books, Inc.).

24. J.T. Gibbs, (ed.) *Young, Black, and Male in America* (New York: Auburn House, 1988).

25. Ibid.

26. Barri Ronald Flowers, *Minorities and Criminality* (New York: Greenwood Press, 1988).

27. Barrett, "Homicide and Suicide."

28. Ibid.

29. J.P. Fitzpatrick, "Drugs, Alcohol and Violent Crime," *Addictive Disease* 1 (1974): 353-367; R. Curt Bartol *Criminal Behavior* (New Jersey: Prentice Hall, 1991).

30. L.E. Gary, (ed.) *Black Men* (Newbury Park: Sage Publications, 1981).

31. *New York Times*, National Edition, "Crack Brings Violence to Areas of New York." October 19, 1987, p. 13.

32. Robert K. Kessler, Ann W. Burgess, and John E. Douglass, *Sexual Homicide* (Lexington, MA: Lexington Books, 1988), 15-32; Kenneth G. Busch, Robert Zagar, John R. Hughes, Jack Arbit and Robert E. Bussell, "Adolescents who Kill," *Journal of Clinical Psychology* 46(4) (1990): 473-485.

33. Miller, "Lower Class Culture as a Generating Milieu of Gang Delinquency."

34. Busch et al., "Adolescents Who Kill."

35. Kessler et al., *Sexual Homicide.*

36. Poussaint, "Black on Black Homicide."

37. F.E. Zimring, "Youth Homicide in New York: A Preliminary Analysis," *The Journal of Legal Studies* 13 (January 1984): 81-99.

38. Gibbs, *Young, Black and Male in America*; Barrett, "Homicide and Suicide."

39. J. Kunjufu, *Countering the Conspiracy to Destroy Black Boys* (Chicago, IL: African-American Images, 1985); H.R. Madhubuti, *Black men: Obsolete, Single, Dangerous?* (Chicago, IL: Third World Press, 1990).

40. Lonnie H. Athens, *The Creation of Dangerous Violent Criminals* (London: Routledge, 1989); Rose and McClain, *Race, Place and Risk.*

41. Hugh D. Graham and Ted R. Gurr, *The History of Violence in America: Historical and Comparative Perspectives* (New York: Bantam Books, 1969).

Pastoral Counseling With African American Men

Edward P. Wimberly

Pastoral counseling with African American men focuses on a holistic understanding of manhood that is rooted in the deepest inner feelings, values, and intentions emerging from a man's life. Through pastoral counseling, the African American male discovers his unique self, his true emotions and feelings, his meaning and purpose for life, and his unique contribution and vocation to the world. He is able to engage in all aspects of life, including the formation of close and intimate relationships with significant others, while taking full responsibility for his own growth and development. Pastoral counseling identifies the sources of his manhood as including his African heritage, the African American tradition of equalitarian relationships and androgenous roles, the penchant for oral styles of communication, the use of Bible stories and characters, and the capacity to be empathic with African American women.

Traditionally, men have been applauded for being more cerebral and less emotional than women. However, this socially acceptable view of non-emotionalism and cool-headedness has done a disservice to men by impeding the full development of an important part of their personality. More importantly, it can impact negatively on their interpersonal relationships, particularly with women.

African American men face many contradictory pressures. On the one hand, they see, hear, and aspire to achieve the dominant images of masculinity held out by the wider society. On the other hand, African American males face, both directly and indirectly, an emasculating pressure which prevents them from achieving the stereotypical images of masculinity. In the 1960s, Erik Erikson observed that there is an effort on the part of the dominant society to subjugate African Americans, particularly African American men. In his book, *Childhood in Society*, Erikson discusses the lack of opportunities afforded many African Americans because the means of achieving identity through certain avenues have been systematically cut off from them.[1] Erikson points out that only three avenues of personhood are held out by society for African Americans:

> Three identities are formed: (1) mammy's oral-sensual "honey child"—tender, expressive, rhythmical; (2) the evil identity of the dirty, anal-sadistic, phallic-rapist "nigger"; and (3) the clean, anal-compulsive, restrained, friendly, but always sad "white man's Negro."[2]

Romney Moseley also discusses the "negative identity" that is foisted on African American youth as a result of poverty, racism, narcotics, and unemployment.[3] These social conditions result in many African American men being incarcerated.[4] Thus, the "negative identity" is perpetuated. There is pressure from within the African American community as well as from the wider society for African American men to act out the "negative identity." Our society needs a scapegoat on which to blame its ills, and young African American males are offered as the sacrifice. The result is a restriction of life choices for a large percentage of African American males.

One major goal of pastoral counseling with African American men is to enable them to achieve wholeness by rejecting the "Sisyphus identity," which could be viewed as the "negative identity." The "Sisyphus identity" is well illustrated in the docudrama "Murder Without Motive: the Edmond Perry Story," which relates the story of a promising honor student who was shot by an undercover policeman in the streets of Harlem in 1985.[5] While attending an exclusive prep-school in New England, Edmond Perry read the myth of Sisyphus. He was struck by the fact that Sisyphus was condemned to repeatedly roll a stone up a hill only to have the stone roll back down the hill just as it neared its destination. Edmond commented that this seems to be the destiny of many African Americans in Harlem. He, too, was ultimately a victim of the Sisyphus mythology.

The Sisyphus myth is the fate held out by the wider society for African American males and females. Covert and overt messages push and pull for African Americans to adopt this role. However, as we have been reminded by countless others, "We are not slaves."[6] Nor do we have to play roles that demean and subjugate us.

The pressure to adopt the "negative identity" is felt by every African American, male and female. Indeed, many African American women have abandoned successful careers because of oppressive harassment or because they were treated as if they embodied the "negative identity." Rather than being regarded as persons with gifts, graces and abilities, they have been regarded as women who have stolen their positions and are not qualified to serve in them. Eventually, many African American women leave their positions because they recognize that their true competence will not be rewarded. Even the so-called "whiteman's Negro" faces this kind of harassment.

It is not intended to further oppress African American women by a one-sided analysis of this problem. However, the focus of this article is on African American men. Pastoral counseling attempts to enable African American men to adopt a different identity. The objective is to present a model of holism whereby African American men can access both the masculine and feminine sides of their identities. In so doing, they can find a basis for becoming whole persons who respond to the world from within rather than reacting to the pressures of the external world.

True selfhood for the African American male involves tapping into the inner source of personhood that transcends wider societal images of masculinity. This is what pastoral counseling seeks to access. It involves: (1) exploring the racial and archetypal sources of African personhood in pre-history; (2) attending to the cultural and oral style of the way African American males relate; (3) examining the stories and myths with which they identify; (4) editing negative plots through the use of Biblical stories and characters; (5) helping African American men develop the capacity to see the world through the eyes of the women; (6) modelling and attending to feelings through self-disclosure; and (7) developing the relational dimensions of pastoral counseling through immediacy.

The theological assumption undergirding this discussion is that we are all created in the image of God, as the creation story tells us in Genesis 1:26. This image contains our infinite worth as creations of God. There is a push from within each of us to realize this image. Pastoral counseling is one means by which African American men can claim their roots and their innermost spiritual source. Indeed, it is in our spiritual relationship with God and with others that we discover our essential identity—that we have a spark of divinity in us that is God's image.

RACIAL AND ARCHETYPAL SOURCES OF PERSONHOOD IN AFRICA

Charles S. Finch, III, a medical doctor and professor of medicine at Morehouse School of Medicine in Atlanta, has examined the history of matriarchy and patriarchy in pre-historic Africa.[7] Relying on twenty-one years of study of comparative religion, mythology, anthropology, archeology, and evolution, he posits that matriarchy undergirds virtually all culture in Africa. Finch bases his analysis on an examination of Egyptian myths, language, and symbols. He illustrates that patriarchy was an inevitable outgrowth of the development of human consciousness related to a number of economic and social factors. He indicates that matriarchy lost ground because it was one-sided, all consuming, and unhealthy in the same way that patriarchy has become today.[8] According to Finch, Africa, particularly Egypt, avoided the split between matriarchy and patriarchy that dominated the rest of the world. He notes that there was a creative reconciliation between matriarchy and patriarchy in lower cultures of the Nile where patriarchy did not overcompensate for the abuses of matriarchy.[9]

The implication of Finch's work is that the archetypal and racial source of African American manhood can be found in the creative tension between matriarchy and patriarchy. In other words, the racial and archetypal inheritance of African Americans is a creative synthesis between the masculine and feminine cultural dimensions. There is an abundance of evidence that the creative reconciliation between the masculine and the feminine has survived in the United States. A review of the literature on African American male and female sex role imagery reveals that equalitarian roles and androgenous learning of roles are very common within the African American community.[10] In actual practice, many African American males share equally with their spouses in decision making. This sharing has often been depicted as deviant pathology by white social scientists who are heavily committed to patriarchal beliefs. Moreover, the literature reveals a healthy flexibility in the performance of roles in the family. This flexibility has enabled the African American family to survive many difficulties in spite of racism.

However, overcompensating patriarchal postures on the part of African American men is a contemporary phenomenon. Many African American men feel torn because of the demands of patriarchy. They feel that they must identify with patriarchy in order to have any kind of identity. Consequently, there is an overcompensation as well as an attempt to distance themselves from the androgenous and equalitarian aspects of their past. African American males are losing touch with their racial and archetypal history by overemphasizing one aspect of their total personhood.

The recovery of the feminine means the recovery of an ancient synthesis between the male and female. Equalitarian and androgenous roles are contemporary manifestations of this ancient reconciliation. Pastoral counselors need to be aware of the cultural heritage of African American males and employ this awareness in their counseling. Recovering a synthesis between male and female aspects of the African American male personality must be distinguished from the forced submission and feminization of African American men by white society. Frances Cress Welsing in *The Isis Papers: The Keys to the Colors* explores her belief that the feminization of the African American male is the result of a deep seated fear of albinism.[11] Albinism is a genetic deficiency rooted in skin melanization where white tends to be dominated by black, brown, red or yellow.[12] Consequently, Welsing suggests that all racism and the feminization of African American males is rooted in the fear of the annihilation of whiteness due to the dominance of the color black.

The emphasis on African American males embracing their femaleness as well as their maleness is not part of the feminization effort of the wider society. In fact, the opposite is called for; namely, for African American males to embrace the African American tradition of equalitarian relationships and androgenous roles. This emphasis emerges out of an empathy for what womanist thinkers call the strength of African American womanhood. This strength derives from identifying with one's own cultural heritage as opposed to distancing oneself from it.[13] The strength of the womanist relies on looking inward to African American culture rather than to the images of masculinity and femininity presented by the wider society.

THE ORAL AND CULTURAL STYLES OF COMMUNICATION

Emerging out of the creative synthesis between male and female is the African American male's penchant for story-telling as a means of creating intimacy. Oral skills have been highly prized historically, both in Africa and in the African American community.[14] African American culture has been characterized as oral rather than ocular. Oral culture is often associated with the feminine, whereas ocular culture is often associated with the traditionally "masculine" qualities of reason, abstract thinking, reading and writing. Thus, oral skills are a carry-over from the creative synthesis of the male and female in African antiquity.

Story-telling as an oral form builds relationships and facilitates bonding. It requires mutual empathy. Both the story-teller and the story-listener must enter the world of the other in order for story-telling to be effective. Both story-telling and story-listening are at the root of African American culture. African American males have a proclivity for story-telling, particularly as a means of self-expression and intimacy.

In conducting marriage enrichment counseling with African American couples, this writer and his wife found the story-telling method to be very effective. During the initial sessions, many men were reluctant to participate because they had a particular image of the popular encounter group movement. They feared that they would have to air their "dirty laundry" in public,[15] and that they would be forced to face emotional and affective areas of their lives which they were not prepared to confront. Eventually, however, these men found that the story-telling method was a comfortable way to express their feelings and to discuss intimate subjects. They also appreciated hearing their wives tell stories that related experiences from their past. Story-telling about meaningful events was the starting point in the counseling sessions. It was gradually expanded to include stories around events that caused pain and hurt. Thus, the story-telling approach drew on an indigenous style of relating that was comfortable for African American men and women. In this way, the forced, direct, emotional expressiveness and openness which is emphasized in verbal-emotional-behavioral models of counseling and psychotherapy was avoided.[16]

Some scholars caution against the reliance on story-telling as a cultural style by African American men. Aldridge, for example, warns that the inclination of African American men toward story-telling may camouflage the lack of intimacy between them and African American women. She notes that verbal facility among African American men makes it easier for them to enter into relationships with African American women.[17] Using a somewhat different perspective, Carolyn McCrary points out that one reason African American men separate talk from behavior is that many of them have been uprooted from support systems including the family, church, and social networks in the African American community.[18] As a result, she observes that talk often becomes a substitute for actual relating.

Indeed, the pastoral counselor must be discerning so as to detect incongruence between the stories men tell and their genuine feelings or behavior patterns. When using the narrative, oral, cultural style, the pastoral counselor needs to begin with and attend to the stories of the male. As soon as a therapeutic relationship has developed, the counselor should be alert to the words as well as the behaviors of the men. One way to move beyond the words that the stories describe to the concrete behavior is to explore the kinds of relationships that African American men have with their spouses.

SOME EFFECTIVE STRATEGIES IN PASTORAL COUNSELING

Examining the Stories that African American Males Tell

In exploring the stories being told in counseling sessions, it is important for pastoral counselors to pay particular attention to their plots. It is crucial to note, for example, whether the plots are tragic and growth-hindering or whether they are hopeful and growth-facilitating. Undergirding many of the stories that African American men tell is a belief that life offers no real opportunities. Often the discrepancy between words and action is rooted in a lack of hope that underlies the lives of African American men.

The example of the young man who referred to his life as resembling that of Sisyphus, the Greek character who was doomed to a life of perpetual rolling stones up hills, is instructive.[19] Sisyphus was never able to change his life because of an abuse committed against one of the leading Greek gods. Although the young man who identified himself with Sisyphus was bright and college and seminary trained, he saw his life as one of tragedy and dead ends. Many counselees see their lives in terms of central stories in the way that this young man did. In fact, many not only identify with the characters in these stories, but also mimetically identify with the plot; in other words, they imitate the plot embedded in the story. A critical element of pastoral counseling, therefore, is to offer these men alternative stories that challenge the existing ones they internalize. In this way, they can begin to embrace alternative plots for their lives.

Editing Stories of African American Males

Pastoral counseling provides a forum for exploring personal stories within the context of divine Scriptures. Scriptural stories in the Old and New Testaments often provide a better vision and future hope for African American males than do Greek tragedies such as that of Sisyphus.[20] Here, too, the pastoral counselor must explore with African American men the Biblical characters and stories with which they have identified. Many African American men, especially the homeless and victims of AIDS, have backgrounds seeped in Biblical stories.[21] These stories, which permeate their lives despite the alienation many feel from the church, have become an important resource for pastoral counseling.

The goal of exploring the biblical stories and characters with African American men is to help them take on the role of the characters with which they have identified. Such role-taking focuses on the power of Biblical characters to shape people's perception of reality, to influence the way people interpret what happens to them, and to provide a vantage point for envisioning hope in the world.[22] The significance of taking on the role of Biblical characters lies in the vision of hope which undergirds Bible stories. Bible stories and their characters move toward a hopeful future despite the abundant hardships and difficulties they face. Such a vision of the future challenges the tragic dimension of scripts such as the myth of Sisyphus. Thus role-taking in pastoral counseling enables African American men to find meaning in their lives through the vision of a hopeful future.

In *Visions for Black Men,* Na'im Akbar proclaims that we should not underestimate the vision shaping potential of Scripture. While he emphasizes the symbolic universality of biblical mythology,[23] he also embraces the idea that those who claim Christianity are part of the same historical stream represented in the Bible. That is to say, African American people were present in the Bible along with all others and were included in God's vision of salvation.[24] Thus, the Bible also has a liberating historical efficacy for freeing African Americans from oppression and mental slavery.

Pastoral counseling encourages African American males to compare their own personal stories with the larger vision embedded in Biblical stories. The aim is to help them edit or re-author their stories in light of this larger vision. In so doing, they embrace their true identities and manhood in the way that many of their foreparents did. Liberation for African American men comes, then, when they re-discover the significance of the Bible for their lives.

Developing the Capacity to See the World Through the Eyes of Women

One major difference between males and females lies in how each views and interprets the world. The way men and women differ in interpreting the world, however, is not limited to the rational/irrational dichotomy often propagated by the dominant culture. Feminist psychologists such as Carol Gilligan have examined gender differences in great detail.[25] These differences provide the framework for an important theme of this presentation; namely, that part of growing into manhood involves learning to see the world through the eyes of women — our mothers, our sisters, our spouses, and our female friends. The assumption is that African American males are well trained in what makes them male. To become spiritually and emotionally whole, however, they must also recapture the so-called "feminine" side of their personalities.

Many African American men are afraid to attempt to see the world through the eyes of women. At issue is the dominant images of what it means to be male and female in this culture. However, the value of trying to see the world through the eyes of African American women is that it may lead to personal wholeness for both males and females.

More importantly, such an effort could help restore the creative synthesis between maleness and femaleness that is part of our racial and ethnic heritage. Womanist thinkers have shown that many African American women derive strength from their cultural and religious heritage.[26] These scholars have shown that African American women place more emphasis on being connected with their heritage than on the expectations of wider society. A rediscovery of this way of life will put African American men in touch with their historical and religious roots.

Pastoral counselors need to be aware that helping African American men see things through the eyes of women has the potential of enabling them to discover hidden aspects of their essential personality in its wholeness. This counseling is best accomplished in group settings.

Self-disclosure and Immediacy

Self-disclosure is a technique whereby the counselor facilitates the involvement of the group in telling stories about their own lives. By giving an example of what is expected, the counselor provides a model of what to do and how to do it. Modelling through self-disclosure brings a perspective to the counselees' existing story-telling skills which lends itself to genuineness or authenticity. Self-disclosure is an important aspect of pastoral counseling with African American males.

If the counselor observes any discomfort in the counselees or if the counselees themselves express such feelings at a particular moment in the counseling process, the counselor must immediately address this issue. This is referred to as immediacy. This technique is particularly important when counseling African American males. Failure to do so can be a hindrance to the relationship between the pastoral counselor and the counselee.

SUMMARY

One major theme of this presentation is the recovery to wholeness for the African American man through the rediscovery of the feminine side of his personality. This may be accomplished by tapping into a reservoir that transcends stereotypical images of masculinity and femininity. The sources of this reservoir are the African pre-history of creative synthesis between the masculine and the feminine, the cultural oral style, stories and Scriptures, the capacity to see the world through the eyes of women, and modeling wholeness in pastoral counseling. The hope is that African American men will become full participants in the family, extended family, church, and community networks that are vital sources of this reservoir and of their personhood.

The implications that can be drawn from this article relate to the cultural and religious heritage of African Americans. This article has defined the fundamentals that shape manhood in the African American community. Valuing this heritage as well as sanction-ing the appropriation of it is essential. In developing a macro-picture for the ills facing African American men, it is important to acknowledge the role of micro-facilitating strategies which take place in the religious life of the community, in families, and in pastoral care and counseling. These micro-strategies include Bible reading, participation in religious ritual and activities, story-telling and story-listening, pastoral counseling, and face to face relationships. Such micro-strategies are the building blocks for personhood.

NOTES

1. Erik Erikson, *Childhood and Society* (New York: W.W. Norton, 1963), 241–246.
2. Ibid., 242.
3. Romney M. Moseley, *Becoming a Self Before God* (Nashville: Abingdon Press, 1991), 70.
4. See Gayraud Wilmore, editor, *Black Men In Prison: The Response of the African American Church* (Atlanta: ITC Press, 1990).
5. This docudrama aired on NBC, January 6, 1992.
6. Carolyn McCrary makes reference to Howard Thurman's saying in "Interdependence as a Norm for Pastoral Counseling" (STD Dissertation, Interdenominational Theological Center, 1989).
7. Charles S. Finch III, *Echoes of the Old Darkland: Themes from the African Eden* (Atlanta: Khenti, Inc., 1991), xiii.
8. Ibid.
9. Ibid., 110–111.
10. Walter Allen, "The Search for Applicable Theories of Black Family Life," *Journal of Marriage and the Family* (1978): 117–129; Diane Lewis, "The Black Family Socialization and Sex Roles," *Phylon*, 36 (1975): 221–237; Bernadette Gray-Little, "Marital Quality and Power Processes Among Black Couples," *Journal of Marriage and the Family* (1982): 633–646; and Leland Axelson, "The Working Wife: Differences in Perception Among Negro and White Males," *Journal of Marriage and the Family* 32 (1980): 457–464.
11. Frances Cress Welsing, *The Isis Papers: The Keys to the Colors* (Chicago: Third World Press, 1991), 86.
12. Ibid., 83.
13. For a discussion of how African American women have embraced their cultural tradition more than African American men, see Katie G. Cannon, *Black Womanist Ethics* (Atlanta: Scholars Press, 1988), 87–88.
14. Edward P. Wimberly, *African American Pastoral Care* (Nashville: Abingdon, 1991).
15. See Patricia Boyde-Franklin, *Black Families in Therapy: A Multisystems Approach* (New York: Guilford, 1989), 18–20 for a discussion about the reluctance of African Americans to air dirty laundry in public.
16. Edward P. Wimberly, "Black Issues in Psychology," *Dictionary of Pastoral Care and Counseling* (Nashville: Abingdon, 1990), 96–98.
17. Delores P. Aldridge, *Focusing Black: Male and Female Relationships* (Chicago: Third World Press, 1991), 56.
18. See Gayruad Wilmore, *Black Men in Prison: The Response of the African American Church* (Atlanta: ITC Press, 1990), 27–29.
19. Edward P. Wimberly, "Spiritual Formation in Theological Education," *Advances in Clergy Assessment and Career Development* (Nashville: Abingdon Press, 1990), 27–31.
20. For a discussion of the significance of Scripture in the development and growth of African American males see Na'im Akbar, *Visions for Black Men* (Nashville: Winston-Derek Publications, Inc. 1991), 43–62.
21. The writer's wife directed a day shelter for homeless people in Evanston, Illinois for two years. During that time the writer was very involved with working with homeless people in pastoral counseling. He also worked with a support group for AIDS workers who often found that African American AIDS victims used Bible stories, characters, and songs as a resource for sustenance during their battles with AIDS.
22. See Thorvald Kallstand, "The Application of the Religio-Psychological Role Theory," *Journal for the Scientific Study of Religion* 26 (1987): 367–374; Donald Capps, "Sunden's Role-Taking Theory: The Case of John Henry Newman and His Mentors," *Journal for the Scientific Study of Religion* 21 (1982): 58–70.
23. Akbar, *Visions of Black Men*, 21.
24. For a discussion of Black people's presence in the Bible see Cain Hope Felder, *Troubling Biblical Waters: Race, Class, and Family* (Maryknoll, New York: Orbis Books, 1989).
25. Coral Gilligan, *In a Different Voice: Psychological Theory and Women's Development* (Cambridge: Harvard University Press, 1982).
26. Boyde-Franklin, *Black Families in Therapy*; Aldridge, *Focusing Black: Male and Female Relationships*.

The Role of African American-Owned Radio In Health Promotion: Community Service Projects Targeting Young African American Males

Phylis Johnson and Thomas A. Birk

African American radio stations serve as change agents by encouraging community partnerships, with particular emphasis on educating and influencing young African American males, parents, teachers, and school administrators. This study was part of a larger project designed to investigate community service activity at culturally-specific radio stations owned by African Americans. These stations were found to promote drug awareness, non-violent behavior, education, and other "health" issues most likely to impact African American male youth.

For more than a half century, African American radio has succeeded in establishing community partnerships and has served as a change agent for political, economic, and social empowerment. Now on the 25th anniversary of Martin Luther King, Jr.'s death, African American radio continues its plea for change to a new generation of young African American males. In doing so, African American radio has become an important delivery system in the urban community. Best notes:

> The key to effective action is the recognition that our delivery system is as important as the context of health promotion interventions, if not more so, and critical if . . . health promotion research is to achieve significant national impact.[1]

The Secretary's Task Force on Black and Minority Health published by the U.S. Department of Health and Human Services calls for partnerships between local health agencies, law enforcement agencies, schools, and community organizations.[2] Health educators and researchers too have urged communities to create a support network for African American male youth using traditional and non-traditional communication delivery systems such as families, schools, churches, small businesses and the media.[3]

Mass media has often functioned as an adversary to health promotions in the inner city, with numerous alcohol and cigarette advertisements specifically designed to entice young

African American men to experiment with these habit-forming substances.[4] For this reason health-care advertising by the mass media has been less effective in providing useful health information to these youth than interpersonal sources such as the family, friends, and school.[5] Mass media has failed to influence public policy over the years because its role has been solely "one of civic mobilization,"[6] rather than one of inspiring government or community action. Reese and Danielian observed that it is national media leaders who set the agenda on public policy, not the smaller media organizations.[7]

Alcalay and Taplin criticized mass media in general for its failure to connect to the community and its neglect of "cultural, economic, demographic and health priorities."[8] A national study of African American and minority health concerns in the 1985 and 1986 Heckler reports found that young African American men were most at-risk for drug abuse and homicide, and that the success of health campaigns dealing with these issues was dependent on the ability of delivery systems to change the social and political environment in the community.[9]

Culturally-specific media, in particular African American radio stations, have been a social and political force nationwide for almost a half century,[10] empowering young African American men to participate politically and economically in their communities, encouraging community participation in education,[11] organizing voter registration campaigns,[12] and providing cultural events and family unification.[13] The success of African American oriented radio stations (many of which are owned by African Americans) is indicated by their large audience shares in many cities, as documented by a variety of trade publications.[14] As a community leader in urban neighborhoods, African American radio has fought drug related street crime,[15] has brought together gang leaders to openly discuss solutions to community violence, and has generated money and supplies for a number of non-profit organizations, local police departments, social agencies and schools.[16]

URBAN RADIO CONNECTS WITH AFRICAN AMERICAN MALE YOUTH

The 1985 Heckler report urged greater cultural sensitivity by the media when dealing with health-related issues of young African American men. Specifically, the report suggested that targeted media campaigns should be conducted. One year later, the 1986 Heckler report identified urban violence, homicide, drug-related behavior, and absenteeism from school as being highly significant and interrelated health risk factors for African Americans, particularly males under 35 years of age.

The impact of these emerging situations in urban environments was discussed by Amuleru-Marshall who observed that 50 percent of all homicides have been linked with abuse of alcohol and other drugs by the highest at-risk age group, 15- to 24-year-olds.[17] Firearm homicide is now the second leading cause of death among teenage African American males,[18] and these rates are increasing disproportionately among these youth, particularly in metropolitan areas. Alcohol and substance abuse, poverty, racism, access to firearms, and the "cultural acceptance of violent behavior" (e.g., domestic and gang violence) have been identified by the Centers for Disease Control as the underlying causes for the rise in violent crime.[19]

Other minority health issues, identified by the Heckler Report as most likely to be affected by health education interventions were: smoking, teenage pregnancy, sexually transmitted diseases, child abuse, stress management, diet and exercise.[20] African American owned radio addressed some of these concerns to a lesser extent than those dealing with alcohol and substance abuse, gang violence, and school attendance. The literature suggests that many of these "other" issues originated from the breakdown of the African American family and consequently, African American radio has promoted the reunification of young African American males to their family, church, and community rather than focusing solely on the societal outcomes.

The key ingredient to any effective health education or promotion is community participation and intervention, as opposed to mere awareness.[21] The message must be relevant if it is to inspire involvement and action from young African American males. Harvey and his colleagues observed:

> Wherever meaning accrues, there is education. This may happen in school, at home, in church, on the playground, or in any dimension of the child's life.[22]

This meaning might evolve through the establishment of community leaders or role models, as in the case of Baltimore's WXYV-FM. As Program Director Roy Sampson commented, "All our air personalities are very active in this community. We all have the philosophy that good role models are very important today."[23] Harvey et al. stressed the importance of role models from inside or outside the community to spend time with African American male youth. These researchers felt that "it seems to be the only answer" to drug abuse.[24] Since young African American male teens appear to be strongly influenced by the electronic media which occupies a significant part of their daily routine, the media can provide powerful role models,[25] especially if the medium is culturally-specific.

Thompson and Cusella have credited news stories, rather than planned promotions, for some of the most persuasive messages about drug abuse (e.g., drug-related deaths of movie stars and famous athletes).[26] In some African American radio stations, news reporting has become personal, persuasive and proactive, rather than passive. For example, in 1990, Lee Marshall, news director of then all-rap music station KDAY-AM/Los Angeles, aired "street language" news stories about inner city people victimized by gangs, drugs and other street violence, which specifically attracted the attention of young African American male teens, especially those involved in drug- and gang-related violence.[27] Marshall explained,

> We're not going to stop kids from doing drugs by showing them an egg cooking in a frying pan. Reality to these kids is showing them another kid drowning on his own vomit after using drugs, or a dead kid being put in a body bag. They can relate to that no matter how harsh we might think it is. Nothing is sugarcoated for us these days.[28]

Substance abuse awareness campaigns, as well as other public communication campaigns, have not been as effective as those that allow members of the neighborhood to participate or intervene in the actual prevention programs.[29] As indicated in the literature,[30] the anti-drug and anti-violence community service agenda of African American radio has included the development of interactive community service promotions, such as peer panels and drug-awareness rallies, that have inspired and stimulated participation from young African American males. These panels which often focus on drug-related issues, gang activity, and self-esteem building are moderated by radio personalities with the cooperation of school administrators, parents, and teachers.[31] The management of KMJM-FM, St. Louis was particulary pleased with one panel discussion that brought together an African American male college graduate with an ex-gang member, while a number of urban youth questioned both men about the different paths their lives had taken.[32]

Promotional events, such as teen concerts and guest lectures from radio personalities at area schools, have been organized to send strong anti-drug messages to African American male youth.[33] It was such aggressive anti-drug campaigns that earned WUSL-FM a Presidential Private Sector Award for its community service efforts in Philadelphia.[34] Similarly, WDAS-FM and the Black Entertainment Television network co-sponsored an "anti-drug summit," which brought together several local, state, and federal government officials with 400 Philadelphia youth to highlight the negative impact of street violence and drugs on African American male youth.[35]

Localized programming such as that formated by African American-owned radio has the power to promote community-based health campaigns, particularly those aimed at African American male youth. Its strength comes from its partnerships with parents, teachers, and students, as well as social agencies, politicians, churches, and businesses. Pierre M. Sutton, former president and chairman of the National Association of Black Owned Broadcasters and president of Inner City Broadcasting, remarked that his stations (including the legendary Harlem-based WLIB-AM which was the first Black news/talk radio station in the nation) work towards "developing a unity in the community so that actions can be taken to protect [the] community from itself in many cases. And in other cases from without."[36] Rather than assuming a passive role, as has been fairly typical of mass communication, Sutton's stations have established dialogue with their audience.

STUDY OF AFRICAN AMERICAN-OWNED RADIO STATIONS

The purpose of the study was to assess the commitment and ability of radio, a target audience medium, to reach a particular audience on health-related issues. Data were drawn from a survey of community service promotional activity at all African American-owned radio stations in the United States.

The primary question under study was: How effective can African American-owned radio be in addressing health-related issues in the African American community, particularly those associated with African American male youth? Secondary questions addressed were: What is the frequency of community service promotional activity at these radio stations? What is the nature of the activities? What is the commitment of senior-level management to this activity now and in the future?

Methodology

The Total Design Method (TDM) was utilized in this study.[37] The population was defined as all African American-owned broadcast companies holding licenses for one or more radio stations in the United States. A list of the population was secured from the National Association of Black Owned Broadcasters (NABOB).[38] The information from the NABOB list (i.e., station call letters, address, and the name of the general manager) was compared to the information in the *1991 Broadcasting Yearbook*. Given the nature of the inquiry, the senior operating manager at the *station* level was the person contacted. A total of 96 broadcast companies which held 123 radio stations were included in the study.

A self-administered questionnaire booklet was developed and pretested. The booklet contained 28 questions designed to address the frequency, nature and range of community service promotional activity at the respondent's station or stations. The structure of the questions included a combination of close-ended with ordered choices, partially close-ended, and a very few open ended questions (including a request for comments or additional information on the last page of the booklet).

All materials were mailed in January 1992. Mailings consisted of: a cover letter, questionnaire booklet and a stamped, self-addressed envelope. A simple coding system was developed to ensure confidentiality, but allowed for follow-up mailings to nonrespondents. Several follow-up mailings were sent to nonrespondents.

Results

A response rate of 54 percent of the broadcast companies was achieved. This rate of response is above average for mail surveys when dealing with "'elite' or management-level populations."[39] All but one of the respondents indicated that their stations were involved in community service promotional activity. When asked the number of community service promotions in which the station was involved in 1991, 48.4 percent of the subjects indicated "more than 10," and 17.2 percent indicated "7 to 10." While these statistics are for 1991 only, 79.7 percent of the respondents stated that 1991 was "typical" of the station's level of community service promotional activity. Further, for those subjects who responded that 1991 was not typical, 71 percent indicated the typical level of promotional activity of this nature was "more than 10" annually. When asked about their station's expectations for community service promotional activity over the next five years, 51.6 percent of the subjects stated that it would "increase somewhat," and 29.7 percent of them anticipated that it would "increase dramatically." In other words, 81.3 percent of the managers surveyed stated that they anticipated increasing their community service promotional activity over the next five years.

With regard to the types of community service promotion in which the stations participated, eleven (11) categories, identified in the literature, were listed along with two "other" categories. Participants were asked to indicate *all* that were appropriate. Each of the categories received at least a 10 percent response rate. The largest response category was anti-drug promotion, with 92.2 percent of subjects indicating they were involved in this type of community service promotional activity. All health-related categories and their response rates are shown in Table 1.

Education (26.6% for grades K–12; 15.6% for college) and drugs (21.9%) were the two highest ranked categories in which respondents indicated that the radio station was "most involved." It should be noted, however, that respondents mentioned education most often (39.1%) as the type of community service promotion that was "most successful." Anti-drug promotion, on the other hand, had a much lower response (7.8%).

The literature indicates that African American radio draws huge crowds to its community service promotional events.[40] Further, it is in this environment that station personnel have the best opportunity to be in a face-to-face relationship with the audience, the type of situation, as mentioned, in which the most effective communication typically occurs. Respondents were asked a series of questions which dealt with those promotions in which the audience was required to attend a function outside the home or confines of the station.

TABLE 1
Types of Health-Related Community Service
Promotions Most-Often Mentioned by Respondents

Activity	Percent
Drugs	90 %
Education (Elementary/Secondary)	77
Voter Registration	75
Employment	73
Violence	63
Education (College)	56
Alcohol	52
Housing	50
Parenting	44
Day Care	14

NOTE: Other categories included activities related to AIDS, heart disease and other specific diseases.

Approximately 60 percent of the stations stated that "most" or "all" of the promotions were in the form of an event. When asked the typical attendance at the "best attended" event, a few stations indicated that promotions attracted in excess of 50,000 people (one station indicated over 750,000), but the attendance category most frequently reported by respondents (29.7%) was "1.000 to 2,999." Normal attendance for most respondents (78.1%) was in the category of "under 1,000." The following is a breakdown of the respondents by type of facility: AM station—48.4%; FM station—21.9%; AM/FM Combo—28.1%. A small proportion (1.6%) did not respond. This breakdown of the sample is similar to the way these groupings occur in radio in general. The following three format types dominated these radio stations: Urban Contemporary (48.4%); Gospel (34.4%); and Black Adult Contemporary (25%). Some stations engage in "block program-ming," and, therefore, reported more than one format type.

Discussion

This study was part of a larger project designed to investigate community service activities at radio stations owned by African Americans. The literature is rich with the history of African American radio and its impact on the urban community.

In today's media marketplace, "mass communication" is considered by some to have little relevance as a vehicle for health promotion or public policy changes. Further, mass communication is not viewed as the most significant solution to health problems.[41] Of all of the media, radio is probably the most targeted and competitive, with some eleven thousand stations now on the air. Survival depends on those stations that do the best job of serving their audiences, and a major part of that service today is the station's involvement in promotions which have a direct impact on the wants, needs and desires of their individual constituencies.[42]

This study has shown the pervasive occurrence of community service promotions at African American-owned radio stations. Over 98 percent of these stations reported that they actively engaged in this type of activity. The commitment of these stations was shown by the frequency of these activities as well as their projections for increasing them in the future. Since much of this activity is in the form of events, the opportunity for this medium of mass communication to engage in one-on-one contact (interpersonal communication) with the audience exists naturally.

In their responses to open-ended questions, many subjects indicated that the ideas for a particular promotional activity came from employees who by design or happenstance identified a special need in the community (e.g., at a civic meeting or a news event), and brought it to the attention of the key management personnel who, in turn, developed a promotion to address the need. Further evidence of this came from the actual promotions mentioned by subjects. Table 2 shows a partial list of the most successful promotions identified by the respondents. While some promotions addressed a national problem (e.g., heart disease, sickle cell anemia, or high blood pressure), many were related to community-specific problems that directly affect young African American males.

TABLE 2
"Best-attended" Community Service Promotional Events
Identified by Respondents
(partial list)

Unity Weekend*	Summerfest*
Family Day in the Park*	Juneteenth Celebration
"Boyz in the Hood"	Gospel Fest
Retired Teachers Banquet	School Supply Drive
Black Expo	Black Arts Festival
Push Fund-Raiser	Voter Registration
Saturday in the Park (Drug Awareness)	
Watershed Project (Addressing Poverty)	
Build a Mountain of Food	
Turkey Jam II (raise money to feed the homeless)	

*These promotions, in part, addressed or celebrated the family.

Responses to an open-ended question about promotion type indicate that the respondents recognized and had a concern for the special challenges faced by African American communities, and young males in particular. Some responses included: "I feel if we can educate our own, we can significantly reduce the problems facing our community," "Most organizations and individuals realize the importance of focusing on education and other problems at an early age," and "We attempt to build self-esteem." There also appeared to be a high level of reciprocity from the African American community as evidenced by their attendance at community service promotional events. Audience response was most often mentioned as the criterion used for judging the success of a promotion.

The results from this study show that education, drug awareness, alcohol awareness and specific health problems (or diseases) are among the most common types of community service promotional activity. This is consistent with the education literature[43] which speaks to the need for bonding among at-risk African American male students, and for developing inner-city community partnerships with families, businesses, and the media.

Recommendations For Community Projects

The commitment of African American radio to its listeners and its desire to establish partnerships are expressed through its community service promotional activities over six decades. African American radio has sponsored fund-raising promotions for a number of non-profit organizations, such as YMCA, Big Brothers, United Negro College Fund, March of Dimes, The National Civil Rights Museum and American Cancer Society, as well as local police departments, social agencies and schools (and school-related athletic programs.) These organizations, in particular, have contributed to the physical and social well-being of young African American urban males. The following are some community service events that have worked well for African American stations in metropolitan areas:

1. *Expositions.* Cultural and/or business expos introduce teenage African American males to community leaders and their cultural past.

2. *Family days.* Family unity days may be as simple as holding a city-wide picnic, while others may commemorate Juneteenth Day. Some stations sponsor father and son softball games, and youth groups play against local business leaders and on-air personalities.

3. *School publicity.* African American radio helps promote health fairs, student plays, PTA meetings and parent-teacher days. Administrators and teachers might invite on-air personalities to discuss health issues and urban problems with their students.

4. *Peer panels.* Peer panels bring together African American male youth with community leaders, parents and teachers to discuss school and neighborhood problems.

5. *Youth shows.* Nightly or weekly youth shows highlight urban issues affecting teenage African American males.

6. *Youth events.* Theme concerts such as "Stop The Violence" and "Do The Right Thing: Stay in School" have attracted African American male teenagers in the past, and similar types of events are held in urban communities across the nation.

These types of activities are not new to African American radio, which is committed to improving education and community unity within urban neighborhoods. Indeed, it is a credible source from which to "communicate" non-violent solutions to African American male youth.

CONCLUSION

Based on the results of this study, it can be seen that community service promotion (an important element of which is health-related needs in the African American community) is an active, important, and highly regarded part of the programming at African American owned radio stations. While the literature seems to favor interpersonal communication, especially for African American male youth, their parents, church, school and community, as the important change agent in educating a particular audience on health-related issues, this study suggests that a "mass" (yet targeted) medium such as radio is influential as well. Moreover, this medium has the advantage of reaching many, through a few critical voices; in this case, the voices of African American radio broadcasters. As Fred Brown, Jr., former NABOB Marketing Director has pointed out,

> Our presence is a testimony of five decades of trials and triumphs, struggles and successes. There is at least one NABOB member in almost every urban market in the country. In small

markets, NABOB stations are the sole broadcasters committed to programming music and public affairs geared specifically toward a Black audience, reflecting the cultural sensitivities and concerns of the community at large.[44]

African American radio and other targeted media seem to be an excellent change agent for those issues confronting African American male youth. It is an area that needs further study, especially with regard to its impact on educating young African American males on topical and non-traditional health issues, such as gang violence and homicide. Having served several generations of African Americans for more than half a century, African American radio is now in a position to influence, and perhaps empower, a new generation of African American males. In the words of Coretta Scott King, African American radio has the power and influence to "go beyond the Black community."[45] If this is true, and that power can be tapped, the potentially positive impact on an increasingly multicultural society warrants further study in this area.

NOTES

The authors would like to acknowledge Sharon A. Shrock, Ph.D. for her assistance in the project. She is Associate Professor of Curriculum and Instruction at Southern Illinois University-Carbondale where she coordinates the graduate programs in Instructional Development and Technology.

1. J. Allan Best, "Intervention Perspectives on School Health Promotion Research," *Health Education Quarterly* 16, 2 (1989): 305.

2. "Homicide Among Young Black Males—United States, 1978-1987," *JAMA, The Journal of the American Medical Association* 265, 2 (1991): 183-184.

3. Stephen B. Thomas, "Community Health Advocacy for Racial and Ethnic Minorities in the United States: Issues and Challenges for Health Education," *Health Education Quarterly* 17, 1 (1990): 13-19.

4. Thomas, "Community Health Advocacy for Racial and Ethnic Minorities in the United States."

5. Joey Reagan and Janay Collins, "Sources for Health Care Information In Two Communities," *Journalism Quarterly* 64, 2 & 3 (1987): 560-563, 676.

6. Donald L. Shaw and Maxwell E. McCombs, "Dealing With Illicit Drugs: The Power—And Limits—Of Mass Media Agenda Setting," in Pamela J. Shoemaker,(ed.) *Communication Campaigns About Drugs, Government, Media, and the Public*, p. 119 (Hillsdale, NJ: Lawrence Erlbaum, 1989).

7. Stephen D. Reese and Lucig H. Danielian, "Intermedia Influence And The Drug Issue: Converging on Cocaine," in Shoemaker (ed.) *Communication Campaigns About Drugs, Government, Media, and the Public*, pp. 29-45.

8. Rina Alcalay and Shahnaz Taplin, "Community Health Campaigns: From Theory to Action," in Ronald E. Rice and Charles K. Atkin, (eds). *Public Communication Campaigns* (2nd ed.), p. 106 (Newbury Park, CA: SAGE Publications, 1989).

9. Margaret M. Heckler, *Report of the Secretary's Task Force on Black & Minority Health: Executive Summary 1.* (Washington DC: US Department of Health and Human Services, 1985, 1986).

10. See, for example, Walt Love, "Fifty Years and Counting: Legendary WJLB Keeps on Kickin." *Radio & Records* (15 December 1989): 75-76; and "The Year In Review," *Radio & Records* (20 December 1991): 42.

11. Phylis Johnson, "Black/Urban Radio Is In Touch With The Inner City: What Can Educators Learn From This Popular Medium?" *Education and Urban Society* 24, 4 (1992): 508-518.

12. Personal interview, WDIA-AM Vice President Rick Caffey (February 11, 1992).

13. Family unification days are typical events held by African American owned radio stations. See, for example: Walt Love, "WDAS Brings Philly Together: Twelth Annual Unity Day Focuses on Community, Youth, and Family Fun," *Radio & Records* (27, September 1991): 50.

14. See, for example, Reed E. Bunzel, "AMs Take Five Top Spots In Arbitron: Urban, soft AC formats continue strong showings; CHR, AOR hold steady in fall survey." *Broadcasting* (13 January 1992): 84-85; and see "Urban Soars, News Stations Drop in Birch," *Radio & Records* (14 June 1991): 1, 39.

15. Walt Love, "WVEE Wages War Against Violence," *Radio & Records* (6 December 1991): 36.

16. See, for example, Walt Love, "Civil Rights Museum Debuts," *Radio & Records* (5 July 1991): 39; and also "Summer Fun In The City." *Radio & Records* (20 July 1990): 58.

17. Omowale Amuleru-Marshall, "Substance Abuse among America's Youth." *The Urban League Review* 13, 1&2 (1989/1990): 96.

18. Lois A. Fingerhut, Deborah D. Ingram, and Jacob J. Feldman, "Firearm and Nonfirearm Homicide Among Persons 15 Through 19 Years of Age," *JAMA, The Journal of the American Medical Association* 267, 22 (1992): 3048-3053.

19. "Homicide Among Young Black Males," *JAMA*.

20. Heckler, *Report of the Secretary's Task Force on Black & Minority Health: Executive Summary 1*, 194.

21. Alcalay and Taplin, "Community Health Campaigns: From Theory to Action."

22. William B. Harvey, Paul F. Bitting and Tracy L. Robinson, "Between a Rock and a Hard Place: Drugs and Schools in African-American Communities," *The Urban League Review* 13, 1&2 (1990): 120.

23. WXYV Program Director Roy Sampson cited in Walt Love, "WXYV's Winning Ways," *Radio & Records* (14 June 1991): 48.

24. Harvey, Bitting and Robinson, "Between a Rock and a Hard Place," p. 127.

25. Jane D. Brown, Kim W. Childers, Karl E. Bauman and Gary G. Koch, "The Influence of New Media and Family Structure on Young Adolescents Television and Radio Use," *Communication Research* 17, 1 (1990): 65-82.

26. Teresa L. Thompson and Louis P. Cusella, "Muddling Through Small Wins: On The Need for Requisite Variety," in Lewis Donohew, Howard E. Sypher and William J. Bukoski (eds.) *Persuasive Communication and Drug Abuse Prevention*, pp. 317-333 (Hillsdale, NJ: Lawrence Erlbaum Associates, 1991).

27. Johnson, "Black/Urban Radio Is In Touch With The Inner City."

28. Walt Love, "Ganging Up on Gangs: Radio Fights Crime," *Radio & Records* (5 October 1990): 50.

29. Alcalay and Taplin, "Community Health Campaigns: From Theory to Action."

30. See, for example, Fred Brown, Jr., "African-American Broadcasters: The Link To Their Communities," *The Pulse of Radio: Radio's Management Weekly* 5, 46 (1990): 22-24; Lucia Cobo, "Philly Station Giving Power to the People," *Broadcasting* (7 January 1991): 89.

31. Doug Carroll, "Panel Keeps Youth Talking of Solutions," *St. Louis Post-Dispatch* (21, September 1989): see radio column/section.

32. Robin Boyce, KMJM-FM, St. Louis, Community Service Director gave "Guest Lecture" at Southern Illinois University at Carbondale, April 4, 1991.

33. Walt Love, "Cool Fun In The Summertime," *Radio & Records* (10 May 1991): 48.

34. Cobo, "Philly Station Giving Power to the People."

35. Love, "WDAS Brings Philly Together."

36. "Pulse Interview: Pierre M. Sutton," *The Pulse of Radio: Radio's Management Weekly* 5, 46 (1990): 19.

37. Don A. Dillman. *Mail and Telephone Surveys: The Total Design Method* (New York: John Wiley and Sons, 1978).

38. NABOB, The National Association of Black-Owned Broadcasters (Washington, DC: NABOB, 1991).

39. B. Garrison and M. B. Salwen, "Professional Orientation of Sports Journalists: A Study of Associated Press Sports Editors," *Newspaper Research Journal* 10, 4 (1989): 78.

40. Love, "Cool Fun In The Summertime," and see "12-Year Tradition: WDAS Celebrates Unity," *Radio & Records* (14 September 1990): 97.

41. John E. Merriam, "National Media Coverage of Drug Issues, 1983-1987," in Shoemaker (ed.), *Communication Campaigns About Drugs, Government, Media and the Public*, pp. 21-28.

42. Susan Tyler Eastman and R. A. Klein, *Promotions & Marketing for Broadcasting & Cable* (2nd ed.) (Prospect Heights, IL: Waveland Press, Inc., 1991).

43. Warren Chapman, "The Illinois Experience: State Grants to Improve School's Parent Involvement," *Phi Delta Kappan* (January 1991): 355-357; Janice E. Hale-Benson, *Black Children: Their Roots, Culture, and Learning Styles* (Baltimore: John Hopkins University Press, 1986).

44. Fred Brown, Jr., "African-American Broadcasters: The Link to Their Communities," p. 22.

45. Walt Love, "Keeping The Dream Alive," *Radio & Records* (17 January 1992): 46.

ABOUT THE AUTHORS

RONALD K. BARRETT, Ph.D., is Associate Professor, Department of Psychology, Loyola Marymount University, Los Angeles, CA 90045–2699.

VICTOR E. BIBBINS, Ph.D., is Training Development Specialist, Training Academy, D.C. Metropolitan Police Department, Washington, DC 20032, and Adjunct Professor of Education and Psychology, University of the District of Columbia.

THOMAS A. BIRK, M.A., is Assistant Professor, Radio-Television Department, Southern Illinois University, Carbondale, IL 62901; he has several years experience in management and sales in the broadcasting industry.

VICTOR De La CANCELA, Ph.D., is Senior Assistant Vice President, Grants Research/Development, New York City Health and Hospitals Corporation, New York 10013; and Assistant Clinical Professor, College of Physicians and Surgeons, Columbia University, New York.

LAWRENCE E. GARY, Ph.D., is Professor, School of Social Work, Howard University, Washington, DC 20059.

RONALD D. HENDERSON, Ph.D., is Director of Research, National Education Association, Washington, DC 20005.

PHYLIS JOHNSON, M.A., is Assistant Professor, Radio-Television Department, Southern Illinois University, Carbondale, IL 62901; she has worked in radio in Philadelphia and Houston, and is a Ph.D. candidate in Instructional Technology.

DIONNE J. JONES, Ph.D., is Editor of *The Urban League Review,* and Senior Research Associate, National Urban League Research Department, Washington, DC 20005.

BRUCE H. WADE, Ph.D., is Assistant Professor, Department of Sociology, Spellman College, Atlanta, GA 30314.

GAYLE D. WEAVER, Ph.D., is Assistant Professor, Department of Graduate Studies, The University of Texas Medical Branch at Galveston, Galveston, TX 77555–1028.

EDWARD P. WIMBERLY, Ph.D., is Professor of Pastoral Care, Interdenominational Theological Seminary, Atlanta, GA 30314.